THE ART OF LIVING

THE ART OF LIVING

Aesthetics of the Ordinary in World Spiritual Traditions

by

Crispin Sartwell

STATE UNIVERSITY OF NEW YORK PRESS

Published by
State University of New York Press, Albany

© 1995   State University of New York

For information, address State University of New York Press,
State University Plaza, Albany, NY 12246

Production by Christine Lynch
Marketing by Theresa Abad Swierzoeski

Library of Congress Cataloging-in-Publication Data

Sartwell, Crispin, 1958–
      The art of living : aesthetics of the ordinary in world spiritual
traditions / by Crispin Sartwell.
          p.   cm.
      ISBN 0–7914–2359–X (alk. paper). — ISBN 0–7914–2360–3 (pbk. :
alk. paper)
      1. Aesthetics. 2. Aesthetics—Religious aspects. 3. East and
West.   I. Title.
BH39.S284   1995
111'.85—dc20   94–10610
                                                                          CIP

10 9 8 7 6 5 4 3 2 1

For Rachael,
the artist in my life, and of hers.

Contents

Acknowledgments

I am grateful to Doug Anderson, for insight and influence which is embodied especially in chapter 5, but also throughout; to Jerry Levinson, who first got me into aesthetics, and who remains for me model of how to do it; to John McDermott, for personal and professional inspiration; to Richard Rorty, with whom I first worked through Dewey's aesthetics, and who taught me how to be a philosopher; to Arnold Berleant, Renee Lorraine, and Mara Miller, for their advice on the manuscript, and for general aesthetic right-headedness; to Stella and Judy Thompson (no relation) for all sorts of help; to the folks at 202, and to Alexis Moss and Bendel Wilson, who taught me about the art of living; to the philosophy department at Vanderbilt University—including John Compton, Idit Dobbs-Weinstein, Clem Dore, John Lysaker, John Post, Charles Scott, Don Sherburne, Henry Teloh, Jeffrey Tlumak, and Patricia Yahrmatter—who created an atmosphere in which this work could be nurtured; to the editors of *Philosophy East and West*, *Asian Philosophy*, and *The Journal of Speculative Philosophy*, for permission to include, in revised and extended form, material which first appeared in their pages; and to my parents Joyce and Richard, and my kids Emma and Sam, who made it all real.

Introduction

The first task of this book is to develop a theory of art. The second is to take that theory out into the world and see whether and how it can transform ordinary human experience. Now transforming ordinary experience might seem to be an odd thing to expect from a theory of art. It seems that art is the sort of stuff we find precisely in extraordinary moments and extraordinary places, in art museums, concert halls, poetry books, theaters, and so forth: places which are marked off as zones of the unusual and the exalted. One way of taking a theory of art and letting it transform ordinary experience, then, would be to start looking at the world in the way we look at things in museums: "aesthetically," at a distance, and with veneration. That is not what this book is about. I am much more interested in how ordinary experience might transform our way of looking at things in museums, might show us how to get more passionate, more engaged, more immersed.

It is, finally, immersion that this book is about: immersion in the world. Art in the true sense, I believe, is a way of becoming fully present in the real, a way for people to experience oneness with things and with one another. What makes certain activities arts and what makes certain things works of art, according to the theory developed in the first part of this book, is the capacity of these activities and things to absorb us. And I am using "absorb" here quite literally: what makes these things art is our capacity to merge or achieve fusion with them and their capacity for, their openness to, that fusion. Art is thus something that calls us both into and out of ourselves as and into what is real. Art is the characteristically human way of being in and loving the world. That is what I mean by "the art of living": the process of becoming absorbed into living, of becoming present in one's life.

All of this is to say that art has a spiritual dimension. I do not mean by this that art appeals to us as disembodied spirits; I don't believe in disembodied spirits. I don't mean that art calls us to a higher realm than the physical; I don't think there is any such realm. I mean, rather, that art is human experience at its greatest intensity and its greatest depth. Art is how and what we are in reality; it is what we make of ourselves and our world, or perhaps what our world allows us to make of it. Art, finally, is a way of opening us to, a way of accepting, a way, even, of ecstatically affirming the world in which we abide and the people we are.

This might sound as though art is extraordinary, the creation of the genius, the enlightened soul, the guru. But art is at its most authentic in the most modest and typical forms of human making. Craft, labor, play: such activities, which most people engage in daily, are the truest arts of our culture. My idea is that our enlightenment is to be found precisely where we already are; the idea is not to become artists or appreciators of art, but to realize that we are already artists and appreciators of art. When we are listening to popular music on the radio on the way home from work, we are listening to art that is more typical of and more organically connected to our culture than anything in any museum. When we enjoy a well-designed and written advertisement, when we watch a baseball game on television, when we raise our children with devoted care, when we work with absorption in our gardens, we are authentically experiencing art.

If we could bring this artistry into our awareness, our experience would be transformed. We would continue, perhaps, to perform the very same activities that we are now performing, though we might perform them with an intensified mindfulness. We would not necessarily change anything about the external facts of how we are living. But our appreciation of those facts would be deepened, our commitment to living would be refreshed, our spiritual lives would be animated. We would be "brought to life," brought more fully into the lives we are already living.

In the context of the recent history of Western philosophy of art, such claims sound, to say the least, eccentric. But the roots of this approach in Western tradition and in world traditions run very deep. In addition, a movement is afoot that seeks to free Western aesthetics from its constriction. The works of Arnold Berleant, Ben-Ami Scharfstein, Richard Shusterman, Mara Miller, John McDermott, David Novitz, and Tom Alexander represent, in various ways, an opening of art to life. Most cultures do not distinguish art from craft or from spiritual devotion. Indeed, Western culture did not draw these distinctions until perhaps three hundred years ago. We might interpret this to mean that those cultures, and previous Western culture, simply have or had no art. Or we might interpret it to mean that *we* have much more art than we thought we did. I will mount a case for the latter approach on conceptual grounds, but let me tell you why I really prefer it: it makes our culture and ourselves available to us in a richer, more appreciable way. It gives us a sense of wonder at and gratitude for our own experience and the lives we make together.

Great art has been connected to every great spiritual tradition, because art is always a crystallized devotion to a world in process. The deepest spiritual experiences of many peoples have been, or have been entwined with, the making and using of works of art, or with engagement in absorbing process. This book discusses art in relation to several of the world's great spiritual traditions, including Hinduism, Confucianism, Taoism, Zen Buddhism, and several Native American, African, and African-American traditions. Each of these is used, however, not to explain the art of the culture in question, but essentially to bring us to an awareness of the artistic aspects of ordinary Western experience. What is common to the elements of these traditions that I will discuss is a veneration of the real and a sensitivity to the present moment that yields a heightened celebration of life as we live it.

The book is organized as follows. Chapter 1 formulates and defends a notion of art that seeks to bring art out of the museum and into our everyday experience. This theory describes art as devotion to process and enhancement of experience. The presentation deals somewhat technically with objections, and I ask the reader to bear with me. Chapter 2 develops this notion through the Zen concept of mindfulness and the realization in the Japanese tea ceremony of the transformation of ordinary experience into art. Chapter 3 relates the theory of art developed in the first chapter to the fundamental posture toward life recommended by the *Bhagavad-Gītā,* one of the central texts of Hinduism. This gives the theory its greatest capacity; here "art" becomes simply the way of acting that possesses the most presence and authenticity: the way of life that is consecrated or sacred.

The second part of the book is devoted to directing our attention to neglected or reviled parts of our own culture, which turn out, on reflection, to be our truest art and our truest hope. Chapter 4 discusses the future of the "fine arts" as these are understood within Western culture: the art of the museum and of the avant-garde. I hope that this future is pretty dim. Chapter 5 describes what, from my point of view, is the clearest illustration of the thesis that there is art all around us already: popular music, and in particular blues and country. I suggest along the way that Confucius, if he were around today, would be a country fan. Chapter 6 discusses the use of art as a source of and an example of knowledge, and as a transformative agent in education. Here I try to make more vivid and precise what I mean by such terms as 'absorption,' 'oneness', and 'fusion.' Finally, Chapter 7 describes some of the problems that arise from the form of human making called technology. This chapter presents, through Taoism, a way of rethinking these problems so that we solve them by allowing them to be. More deeply, we solve these problems, and perhaps all real problems, by allowing ourselves and one another to be, and to be artists.

Part One

Opening the Concept of Art

Chapter 1

Process and Product

I

The first thing this book is going to do is attempt to define the term 'work of art.' Now the history of such attempts is anything but edifying. Many definitions have been proposed, and none has stood the test of subsequent (or even previous or contemporary) works of art. Indeed, the sheer conceptuality of the situation is absolutely hopeless. The test of a definition is whether it counts all and only the right items as works of art. That is the only *possible* test of a definition of art; it has got to count as art those items which we all (or at any rate most of us) agree are works of art. Otherwise, the definition could be completely arbitrary. I could, for example, define 'work of art' as follows: anything, and only things, that are crayons or canyons are works of art. Now you might point out that such a definition does not count the *Mona Lisa* as a work of art, and that it does count the Snake River Gorge, and you might point out that these are obviously mistakes. But if my definition does not have to stand up to empirical confirmation, I can laugh off objections like that and stick to my guns.

So a definition has got to be adequate to the facts about which items are, and which items are not, works of art. The problem is this: I cannot, it seems, know precisely which items are works of art and which items are not, until I know what art *is*, that is, until I have a theory or a definition. But I cannot know whether I've got a good theory or definition until I know whether that theory or definition counts all and only the right items. Now this problem is nasty enough when we stick to

Western art and Western thought about art. There are plenty of debates within the Western artworld about whether such works as, say, Piero Manzoni's *Merda d'artista (Artist's Shit)* (a canned and signed limited edition of excrement) are works of art. But the problem gets completely out of hand when one is attempting—as this book attempts—to give a theory that is capable of applying to the art of other cultures, a theory that takes into account the philosophical and spiritual traditions of those cultures. Take, for example, a Navajo sand painting. It more or less *looks* like art, and some sand paintings have been preserved and placed in museums. But the Navajo use sand paintings for purposes they regard as practical and religious. The paintings are used during ceremonies called "sings" to effect cures in persons or in the environment, after which they are usually destroyed. Now the question is: are these items works of art? To know that, we have to know whether a work of art could be intended for practical purposes, or whether there could be art in a culture where the items in question are not preserved. To know *that*, we need a theory of art. But to know whether we've got a good theory of art, we need to know whether the theory has to count Navajo sand paintings. So we're stuck.

And in fact, the entire project of presenting the philosophy of art of non-Western cultures, which is one of the tasks of this book, may seem to be misguided from the start. For notice that art, and for that matter philosophy, are themselves Western notions. It may well be claimed that these concepts have no application to other cultures whatsoever. Let us frame the dilemma this way: there is no way to escape ethnocentrism in a project such as the one reflected in this book. If "we" (Westerners) claim that there is art or philosophy in exactly our sense in, for example, Yoruba culture, then we are guilty of simply slapping our concepts onto their practices in a way that falsifies those practices. All we then experience is Yoruba culture as a pale reflection of our own culture. It is very likely that, in that case, their "art" and "philosophy" will seem to be miserable failures. They will seem to be miserable failures because we judge them by our standards, not theirs. On the other hand, if "we" (Westerners), intent on respecting cultural diversity, deny that our concepts apply at all to Yoruba culture, then we must remain in willful ignorance. We have no equipment to start to investigate other cultures but the concepts we do already possess; we must always start exactly where we are. Simply to deny that our concepts have any foothold in their culture would keep us from trying to understand it at all. At its most extreme, this approach might take the form of simply denying that the Yoruba have any art or any philosophy. That, too, is ethnocentric; since we tend to think of art and philosophy as (potentially, at any rate) among the highest human achievements, denying them to the Yoruba sounds patronizing. So ethnocentrism is inescapable: we are ethnocentric if we apply concepts such as "art" and "philosophy" to other cultures, and ethnocentric if we do not.

This dilemma has immediate implications for how we experience and understand the art of other cultures. For example, the approach of simply slapping our concepts on other cultures has led to specific museum practices. We take an African mask, for example, and encase it in glass in a museum, then we try to appreciate it exactly as we try to appreciate Western paintings. We may be able to appreciate the mask in this way, or we may not. (It's likely that it won't stack up very well with the Monets, works which were consciously projected into the museum context.) But what is missing is precisely the cultural context in which this mask operates: as part of a festival, say: a celebration that includes music, dance, architecture, body decoration, and so forth, and has a very specific religious function. On the other hand, if we *refuse* to bring African masks into our art institutions, because to do so is to falsify them by yanking them out of context, then we may simply be denying ourselves the chance to feel their aesthetic, and for that matter, festive and religious, power. Either way, our experience is impoverished.

The problems that arise here are, to repeat, immediate and practical. The clearest examples of cultures that possess philosophy and art in just our sense are the Far Eastern cultures. But even in China and Japan, the ease with which we identify the moral philosophy, the landscape painting, and so forth is precisely the danger; the apparent familiarity can blind us to the more subtle, but equally important differences. For example, both the philosophy and the art of China are insistently *practical* in orientation. Though there was a brief flourishing of more or less pure abstract reasoning in ancient China, Chinese philosophers have always started with questions such as how rulers are to rule and how a person can live satisfactorily. General questions such as whether it is possible to know anything at all or as to the nature of the Good arise very rarely. Similarly, within the Confucian tradition, music and poetry are valued for the fact that they reflect and effect social harmony, rather than in virtue of the sheer beauty of their form. So when philosophers such as Hsün Tzu make the claim that music is key to the creation and preservation of social cohesion, we are tempted to ignore this as bizarre or dismiss it as hyperbole, rather than hearing it, as it is surely meant, as an absolutely serious discussion of what music is for.

Indeed, the very notion that music is "for" anything at all rings strangely in contemporary Western ears. The modern West has learned to treat art as merely interesting form: lines and colors, masses and surfaces, harmonies and rhythms. We gaze at paintings in museums or listen to symphonies in concert halls in order to have an "aesthetic experience," or to cultivate the "aesthetic attitude." Such an experience has been described by Kant as "disinterested pleasure," and such an attitude has been described by Bullough as "psychical distance." These phrases, which capture the central modern Western view about how art is to be experienced, rely precisely on a contrast of the aesthetic and the practical; much of this book is devoted to putting that contrast into question. The proper response to a painting of a nude, for example, is not supposed to be sexual arousal, but a sheer appreciation of form.

Now this can lead us to two possible reactions. We could simply deny that Confucius and Hsün Tzu are writing about art in our sense. Or we could allow the experience of their writings to affect our own experience of the Western conception of art. It is the latter which I want to suggest is the most promising response: we can hold our concepts, and ourselves as users of those concepts, open to the experience reflected in the expressions of other cultures. We can only start where we are. But where we are can change as we travel. All we can do is muddle through, trying to reach a mutual adjustment of concepts. For example, as we read and take seriously the Confucian notion of music as an agent of social change and cohesion, we might notice with surprise that music *does* play that role in our culture. (I will discuss this at length in the chapter on American music.) To be identified as someone who likes heavy metal, or punk, or rap, or "alternative," or "classic rock," is to be identified with a certain generation and a certain sub-culture. These styles of music affect dress, recreation, and many other aspects of cultural life and expression. They unite people in dance and at concerts and as listeners to the same radio stations; they are important elements of cultural identification and personal self-image. Potentially, then, a reading of the Chinese sources has redirected our gaze to items, and features of those items, that have been neglected in Western philosophy of art. We have learned something about ourselves by taking others seriously.

Such problems run even deeper with regard to other cultures. In subcontinental Indian, many African, and many Native American cultures, for instance, there is not only no distinction between the practical and the aesthetic; there is no distinction between art, philosophy, and religion. In one sense, for example, the Indian tradition in philosophy is both the most ancient and the most elaborate in the world. In another sense, however, there *is* no Indian philosophy, at least until very recently; virtually all Indian thought, including reflections on what we call their art, are in the service of religion. Indeed, virtually all of their *art* is devotional in a broad sense; what we are tempted to identify as their sculpture, their literature, their dance, even their architecture: almost all of it is permeated by religious concerns and religious purposes. The spiritual classic *The Bhagavad-Gītā*, to which I devote a chapter of this book, is a passage from the great Indian epic *The Mahāb-*

hārata. Is *The Mahābhārata* a work of fiction in which a great scripture is embedded, or is it through and through a religious work? Within traditional Indian vernacular, that question cannot even be formulated.

In fact, one thing that emerges from a study of the world's art is that most of it has been produced for religious reasons. African masks and music usually have a function within religious festival. Navajo sand paintings are used for healing, and, beautiful and elaborate though they are, are destroyed when their task is accomplished. Are such sand paintings medicines, or works of art, or both, or neither? Again, the approach I suggest to such questions is, first, to admit that they cannot be solved on their own terms, and then to start trying to muddle through. Notice, for example, that for thousands of years most Western art, too, was produced for religious reasons. Notice that, in the West, we continue to produce stained glass for churches, continue to compose gospel music, and so forth. That is, much Western art continues to be devotional in character. And notice, too, that we approach our museums themselves in an attitude of devotion, that we still attribute to works of art and to artists an odd sort of supernatural, and perhaps healing power. We still speak of artists, for example, as "inspired," surely an acknowledgment of their quasi-religious function. And the paintings of Van Gogh, for example, seem to be imbued with a life and a value that is essentially magical: we do not treat these items simply as inanimate objects, paint on canvas; we venerate them, and exchange them for millions of dollars. Again, we see how a serious encounter with the practices of other cultures might affect our experience of our own. It might even lead us to count as art things which we had previously neglected.

No non-European culture has a concept of "art" in the aesthetic sense, and no culture has the practices of display and preservation that attend that concept. (This point must be handled with care with regard to Japanese and Chinese culture.) However, it is also true that Europe itself only developed this concept in the eighteenth century, and that the aesthetic concept of art built on and refined a sense of 'art' that meant 'devoted skill.' In fact, *that* sense of 'art' is still current in Western languages. One might say of a baker, for instance, that "he is a real artist," meaning not that his cake ought to be in a museum or ought to be contemplated disinterestedly (indeed, it ought to be devoured), but simply that he displays great skill and devotion in his line of work.

The ancient Greek term for this is *technē*, and it ought to be pointed out that reading "ancient Greek aesthetics" such as Aristotle's *Poetics* raises precisely the same problems as reading the "aesthetics" of non-Western cultures. At any rate, though no other culture has a concept of art in the aesthetic sense, *every* culture with which I am acquainted has a concept of skilled and devoted making. The Chinese, for example, call it *shu*, the Indians *śilpa*, and so forth. Such terms, like our term 'art' in its original sense, do not distinguish between fine art and craft, between fine and decorative art, between fine and applied art. They do not pick out a certain range of activities, materials, mediums, or products. Rather, they characterize a *way* that *any* human activity can be pursued: with great devotion and great skill.

It is not hard to see why items produced this way, and the people who produce them, should be held in veneration in all cultures. Great skill and devotion is always valuable and impressive in itself. And its products are particularly effective in doing what they are intended to do, and particularly satisfying to use. Further, they are particularly pleasing to the gods, whatever gods there may be. Thus, art understood in its most general sense, art as skilled and devoted making, might be something we find wherever human beings are found, and something that is used for whatever human beings use things for. These are not conclusions that can be reached by an armchair examination of the Western aesthetic conception of art. They are, rather, conclusions that can be reached by an attentive experience of the things people make in various parts of the world, and an attentive experience of their reflection on those things.

The theory of art that I am going to go on now to articulate is my attempt to "muddle through." It is my attempt to countenance and celebrate as art as much as possible of what is made with devotion in as much as possible of the world. It is not free of values; it is not a pure description of what is. It is, rather, an attempt to direct the reader's gaze to what I find worthwhile, and it is an attempt to share with the reader an experience I might describe as devotional or spiritual. By 'spiritual,' to repeat, I mean the sharing of human experience at depth: the experience of peace in the world. Finally, I mean peace *through* the world, peace as a result of immersion and identification with the world as a whole. This, I think, is the deepest function of art wherever it appears, and whether it expresses itself religiously, aesthetically, or technologically.

II

One lesson to be derived from the history of attempts to define the word 'art' is that there is no one purpose for which all and only art is made, and no one manner in which all and only art is appreciated. Candidates for an overall artistic purpose have included the imitation and idealization of the real world, the expression of emotion, and the creation of significant form. Theories of art that focus on appreciation have appealed to art as a source of edification or catharsis, or as a source of aesthetic experience construed in terms of distance or nonpractical absorption. Such definitions can be refuted by the flick of a counter-example, particularly from a perspective that includes the avant-garde art of this century. Abstract art cannot be accounted for on the view that art is imitation; horrific or ugly art cannot be accounted for on the view that art is idealization; minimalist works cannot be accounted for on the expression theory; ready-mades and other appropriations from everyday life cannot be explained by formalism. And such theories too, as we shall see, fail miserably in the light of non-Western artistic and spiritual traditions. Much, if not most, of the world's art has been created for purposes that could be described as strictly religious or even magical. Some great art has been made as political propaganda (thirties American leftists), or as moral lessons (Hogarth). No doubt some great art has been made to get the money or the girl. Pop art and Dada ridicule a distanced attitude; *Guernica* does not edify; wrapping islands in the manner of Christo does not provide catharsis. Such considerations have led directly to the claim that 'art' cannot be defined, that there are no necessary and sufficient conditions for something to count as a work of art.[1]

Certain contemporary thinkers have replied that, though there is indeed no one purpose for which all art is made or way in which all art is appreciated, necessary and sufficient conditions for arthood can still be formulated by specifying the relation that works of art display to the institutional or historical contexts out of which works of art arise or into which they are projected. Dickie's institutional theory and Levinson's historical theory are exemplary in this regard. Putting it very roughly, Dickie's view is that an item is a work of art if and only if it has a certain place in the institutional context of the artworld, and Levinson's is that an item is a work of art if and only if it is intended to be regarded in ways that past works of art have been correctly regarded.[2] (I quote their precise formulations in chapter 4.) Now in fact I think such theories, particularly Levinson's, bid fair to provide necessary and sufficient conditions for something to count as a work of art in a certain restricted sense, that is, to identify properties that all and only examples of what are accounted the fine arts display. Nevertheless, even if such theories are successful in this regard, it is still possible to be dissatisfied with them from the point of view of the tradition of art theory. This is because such theories do not tell us, in a general way, why we should care about whether any given item falls within the extension of 'work of art,' that is, they do very little indeed to elucidate the *value* of art in general, which is exactly what traditional theorists have seen as their central task. To say that works of art are items that have a certain relation to the institution of the art world (Dickie), or to past works of art (Levinson), is intrinsically interesting. But the creation of art seems to be something of a universal impulse. It is even plausible to assert that no human culture has been completely anartistic.[3] This seems to indicate that art is in some way central human to human experience, that making art satisfies some central human need. Traditionally one of the functions of art theory has been to relate art to the needs it satisfies, the experiences it reflects or embodies. The institutional and historical theories do not perform this function.

There is, in the tradition of theorizing about art, an alternative to theories that define art in terms of the purposes they serve and the relations they bear to institutions or art history. I have in mind theories that characterize works of art by the distinctive processes that give rise to them and to which they give rise, or by the relation of such processes to the ends for which they are pursued. This chapter presents a new such theory. There are several process theories, all of which are related in various ways to the view I will propound. For example, the idea that art is a form of play, associated with Schiller, is a process theory. And Wollheim develops at least the beginnings of such a theory in *Painting as an Art*.[4] The position that is most closely related to the present proposal, however, is that formulated by Dewey. According to Dewey, art is an experience that possesses rhythm rather than mere accumulation, consummation rather than mere cessation.[5] In some ways I think this is the most satisfying theory of art that has come to my attention, and I will return to Dewey's view presently and again in chapter 5. Nevertheless, I am dissatisfied with Dewey's view for several reasons. I will mention but one here: the view is extremely vague, and would leave us at a loss to decide in most cases whether a given artifact is or is not a work of art. But it is also worth mentioning one of the great strengths of Dewey's view. Dewey's theory steadfastly refuses, in his terms, to "compartmentalize" art. It holds that art emerges organically out of the conditions of human, or indeed more generally, animal life. It does not alienate art into the rarefied province of an economic and intellectual elite. This feature distinguishes Dewey's theory at least from formalist theories and from the institutional view. I take it to be felicitous, and intend to preserve it in the definition I offer.

III

Here is what I take art to be:

> A work of art is an intersubjectively available product
> which (1) is the product of a process in which, to an
> exemplary degree, some aspects of the process itself
> are pursued for their own sake, and not merely for the
> sake of the end for which the process is undertaken,
> and (2) is of a kind, members of which are themselves
> suited to play a role in such processes.

That is, a work of art is the result of activity in which, whatever
its overall purpose, some of the means of achieving that purpose are to an exemplary degree pursued for their own sake as
well as for the sake of the purpose. And such a work is itself of
a kind suited to play a part in the processes pursued for their
own sake as well as for other ends. For example, painting may
be pursued for reasons having to do with the achievement of
personal ambition, the veneration of God or the state, the
expression or discharge of emotion, the recording of historical
events, healing, the decoration of hotel rooms, and so forth.
Architecture has the purpose of providing shelter and places
of business. Music may be designed to edify, to disquiet, to
challenge the virtuosity of piano players, to provide an occasion to dance, or simply to offend. Sculpture may be an exploration of three-dimensional space, of human sexuality, of
mythology, or of the shape of a particular human head. What
makes the items that are thus produced works of art, however,
is that the manipulation of pigments, the conceptualization of
space to be utilized, the juxtaposition of tones, the carving or
modelling of stone or clay, are regarded by the artist as intrinsically satisfying, as well as adapted for their purposes. The
contemporary painter Audrey Flack writes that "it almost
doesn't matter what you paint. It is what takes place during the
act of painting that matters."[6] And it is not only what takes place
in the act of painting that matters, but what takes place in the
act of experiencing paintings. We may experience paintings in
order to cultivate our sensibilities, impress our acquaintances,

augment our collections. But paintings can simultaneously be experienced for the sake of experience. It is plausible, too, to connect these facts; it is in part because it is created in a process pursued for its own sake that the painting is suited to give rise to such processes. It is absorbing because it was created with care.

One of the functions of art, in other words, is the enhancement of everyday activities. The San people of southwest Africa employ ostrich eggs as canteens. They decorate these items with beautiful designs. The purpose of making a canteen is to carry water—a function of extreme practical value in the desert environment—but the San devote themselves to the decoration of these items in part because such decoration helps make the canteens inherently satisfying to use. And in Western culture, many, if not most, of the utilitarian items we employ are decorated or adorned in various ways in order to enhance the satisfaction pursuant to their use. Think of cars, for instance. If such items are themselves created by an artistic process, then my definition counts them as art.

Dewey's aesthetics described art as human experience of a certain sort: rhythmical, coherent, consummatory. The present theory identifies works of art as the products and occasions of such experience, and furthermore begins to explain how such experience happens: in a devotion to means, to process, in short, to life. For though some of us live for ends, all of us live *in* means: all of us are "in process." Art in this sense re-embeds us in the very experiences we are having, and consecrates the moment in which we are having them. That is how I would like to read Dewey's theory of art, which he constructed with the purpose of recovering the continuity of art experience with normal processes of living. As Dewey says in *Experience and Nature*, "any activity that is simultaneously [means and consequence, process and product, instrumental and consummatory], rather than in alternation and displacement, is art."[7]

The visual artist is a person who is not only endowed with the religious, political, aesthetic, and psychosexual purposes she happens to possess, but also with the desire to handle materials and to think through their handling. It is sometimes thought that an artist has a vaguely defined "artistic impulse" which can come to be expressed through any of several mediums. In general, that is not the case. The artist paints in part because she finds satisfaction is *painting*, that is, in mixing and arranging pigments. It is not a coincidence that the painter uses paint; the manipulation of paint and the working out of various problems that arise in that manipulation are regarded as worthwhile in themselves. The visual artist as she works becomes absorbed not only in a final disposition of her work, not only in the reactions it is designed to provoke, or the causes it is designed to promote. She is absorbed not only in her commission, in the approval of peers or critics or gallery-owners, but in the handling of materials, in the shaping of a thing with her hands. Any artist will, I think, recognize that part of the satisfaction inherent in creating a work of art arises from the solution of problems that arise in its creation, torturous though such a process may be in some respects. And though it has indeed occasionally been torture for writers to write or composers to compose, no artist would be willing to have finished works simply appear on command; working out problems within the chosen medium is precisely what constitutes him as an artist.

Wollheim, in *Art and its Objects*, discusses what he terms the *bricoleur* problem.[8] ('Bricoleur' is French for 'handyman' or 'tinkerer.') The problem is this: why do certain processes and materials become the accredited vehicles of art? The present theory presents a rather straightforward answer to that question: stone and paint, for example, are accredited vehicles of art because they are inherently satisfying to work, and because, worked, they are inherently satisfying to employ in various capacities. They are recalcitrant: that is, they do not immediately or easily assume the shape one desires them to. (Though there is, of course, a scale of recalcitrance; paint and clay, for example, are more easily worked than marble. However, clay is by no means easy to shape into an exemplary vessel, and paint by no means easy to shape into an exemplary fresco. That is, these materials are by no means easy to use in a way that suits the result to play a part in satisfying activities.)

A well-made vessel changes the activity of pouring liquids into something that is inherently satisfying. The recalcitrance of materials provides the opportunity to work them, and requires of the artist expertise in their working. This expertise in turn must be developed, a process which, despite its frustrations, can be joyful simply because these materials *are* satisfying to work. But such materials are not utterly recalcitrant; they are not impossible or extremely difficult to work; they are malleable if one devotes oneself to them. It is precisely such a combination of malleability and recalcitrance, along with a perhaps inexplicable capacity to yield satisfaction in manipulation (a match, as it were, between the qualities of the material and human capacities), that leads such materials to be accredited vehicles of art.

So I would like to treat the handling of materials by visual artists as paradigms of artistic process. But artistic processes are by no means limited to such handling. I characterize artistic process as the entire activity that contributes to and precedes the finished artistic product, that leads to the item being made intersubjectively available, whether such processes are physical, emotional, or intellectual. Such processes generally include some initial emotional impulsion or idea which tries to find embodiment, as well as the visualization of the finished product, or at any rate of the next stage of the physical process. And some arts have stages that need not involve any physical manipulation at all. For example, a composer might invent a melody in her head without any recourse to an instrument, as might a poet a poem. An architect in general does not actually make the building she designs with her own hands; nevertheless, there certainly is a process in which the design is generated. Likewise, I do not wish to limit the notion of "product" to portable artifacts. Some artistic processes issue in artifacts, others in performances, plans, interactions, victories (think of chess). I treat the notion of "product" here roughly as any intersubjectively available result of an artistic process. Nevertheless, if a process that is pursued for its own sake does not yield such an intersubjectively available item, however ephemeral or physically discontinuous, it does not yield works of art in the present sense, though we may in a slightly extended sense still call the activity, pursued in that way, an art. One cannot be a poet *only* in virtue of one's mental processes; in order to count as a *work* of art, the poem must be externalized, though before it is made intersubjectively available, it is a potential or proto-work.

IV

A word is in order about what it to pursue an activity for its own sake. I do not mean such a notion to indicate a concept of noninstrumental value of a kind that Dewey, for example, would find objectionable. After all, I am allowing that in every case some end or ends is or are in view in artistic production. Such ends include those delineated in the traditional theories of art, including the imitation or idealization of the real, the expression of emotion, and so forth. They may also include the accumulation of fame or wealth. Certainly they include devotional, religious, and magical ends. Such ends may in some cases be instrumental to yet other ends, and so forth. So I am not arguing that art is nonpractical in any sense. However, Dewey speaks of art providing experiences that are "enjoyable in themselves" or "directly enjoyable,"[9] and I am asserting that artistic process embodies such experiences. However, I think that 'enjoyable' is not the most felicitous term since, again, artistic process is not always an unalloyed delight. One can pursue a process for its own sake even if the process is not purely pleasurable. Furthermore, the opposition between activities performed for their own sake and those performed for an end needs to be thrown quite generally into question, for to devote oneself to the means of achieving an end, in general, both increases the effectiveness with which the end is realized and embeds one more deeply in the process of achieving it. I will return to this point in a discussion of beauty in chapter 3.

Here is an example of what it means to pursue an activity for its own sake, and an example of the aesthetics of the ordinary. The American aesthetician Horace Kallen, writing under the influence of Dewey, describes laborers working on a street with picks and shovels:

> They do it, not because it is their way of living their lives, but because it is their way of earning their livings. They pick and they shovel intermittently, slowly, without zest, without eagerness. The slightest occasion is enough to stop their work, and they return to it reluctantly, as if forced. They appear to be at once bound to it and in flight from it, like an animal tethered. . . . When the five o'clock whistle blows they stop with an incomparable promptness, with every sign of bonds loosened, burdens dropped. They have stopped earning their livings and are ready now, perhaps, to start living their lives.

But if you watch carefully, says Kallen, you may see a surprising thing:

> [E]very so often you will notice a change. Here a man with a pick, there a man with a shovel, will begin to make his movements, you can't tell how or why, in a different way. The intermittency, the slowness, the clumsiness pass over into a smooth continuous rhythm: tool and man seem no longer externally attached but inwardly confluent and shaping a melody of action patterns between the pounding pavement and the sky. . . . Interruptions are now interference, not relief, obstacle, not liberation. . . . [E]arning one's living and living one's life have for the moment compenetrated and become the same.[10]

Kallen goes on to assert that the experience of the second workman is aesthetic. And he might also have claimed—accurately, I believe—that the second workman was engaged in the creation of a work of art: a dance that repairs the city streets. But notice that the workman's activity is obviously not purposeless, that the value of repairing city streets well is hardly noninstrumental. And notice that well-repaired city streets enhance and transform the activity of driving.

It may well be asked, however, how we are to discern that someone is pursuing a process for its own sake. Well, in this case, the character of *Kallen's* experience of the workman's activity changed, as the workman's activity did likewise. That is, the workman's activity was of a sort that transformed a viewer's experience of that activity; exactly as the second clause of the present definition might lead us to predict. I think we *can* often recognize (though perhaps we cannot always tell how) when someone is engaged in an activity for its own sake. And it seems to me that each person is, at least sometimes, in a position, on reflection, to determine whether he is himself undertaking such a process. To put the point in the first person, it seems to me that I am sometimes in a position to say truly whether I am pursuing a process for its own sake or not. This is not, of course, to say that such judgments about my own reasons for pursuing a process are incorrigible; I may be subject to various mistakes here, various forms of self-deception. I am asserting merely that on some occasions reflection can make it evident to me that I am engaged in a process for its own sake as well as for the sake of further goals.

I think of "absorption" as a mark of such a process. We are all familiar, I think, with experiences in which we "lose track of time," absorbed in some process with which we are involved. This book is devoted to using such experiences as a model for how life could be lived. There is a continuum from processes that are experienced by those who undertake them as merely tedious, uninteresting, or mechanical, to those that are paradigmatically artistic, that are to an exemplary degree absorbing.

The standards by which we make such judgments, in other words, are rough and corrigible, but it certainly does not follow that we cannot make more or less reasonable judgments along these lines. Deciding whether or not some product is a work of art, on the present view, requires an examination of the psychological states of its maker and its (potential) experiencers, and this may itself seem to render the application of the definition to particular items problematic. I will have a bit more to say about this later, but for now we can note that there is no particular reason to think that the attribution of subjective states of the kind in question here (if these states *are* properly termed 'subjective,' which I doubt: they are states of persons in relation to things) is any more problematic than the attribution of subjective states in any other case. I am often in a perfectly good position to determine whether you are angry, or depressed, or, for that matter, absorbed. We have all "seen" that someone is absorbed in some process; there are features of behavior which mark persons as being in that state. If we can justify such an ascription to someone in virtue of behavior (including first-person reports), we are in a position to determine whether the process that person is pursuing is artistic.

Now I will argue that no process is *by nature* completely without absorbing elements, that it is possible to work oneself into a state in which one can become absorbed in any process. Finally, I will argue that one's life as a whole could be such a process. But there is no doubt that some processes have more potential for yielding absorption than others. For example, long days spent on the assembly line, performing a repetitive task for the sheer purpose of making a living wage, is likely to be a tedious, anartistic process, whereas crafting a beautiful object, and using such an object in the sort of activity for which it is designed, are likely to pursued lovingly. However, the experience of production-line labor, if it could be engaged in for its own sake, might yield a particularly intense satisfaction, precisely in the overcoming of obstacles to becoming fully present within the activity.

The notion of a continuum of processes is one way of showing the connection of art to everyday life. The present view does not neatly separate the world into those items that do and those that do not count as works of art. Rather, there is a continuum of processes from those that yield products that are clearly not art to those yield products that are paradigmatically so. Art shades off indistinguishably into non-art, and, furthermore, any activity can, in principle, be pursued as an art. It is in these senses that the present view provides an answer to "compartmentalized" views of art.

That said, however, I think that there are distinctive aspects of what are termed the fine arts that fit them to serve as particularly clear cases of art in general. That is why I have included in the definition the notion that a work of art is *to an exemplary degree* created by a process pursued for its own sake. There are two dimensions in which such degrees of absorption can differ. First, of two processes both of which are absorbing, one may be more absorbing than another. I think that what I take to be clear cases of artistic process—such as the arrangement of pigments or the carving of stone—are peculiarly suited to yield an intense satisfaction. Second, the definition counts as art what is created by a process *some aspects of which* are pursued for their own sake. But such processes differ as to the number of such aspects, and the number of aspects which are not so regarded. In a paradigmatically artistic process, most, if not all of the aspects of the process are absorbing. The less the process involves merely tedious aspects, the more artistic it is. Thus, again, to the extent that the definition is capable of picking out what we usually think of as the fine arts, it does so because the processes involved in the fine arts are to an exemplary degree absorbing, and thus because the processes themselves in which they are created and employed are paradigmatically artistic.

Now there are two obvious ways in which this view might be attacked. In fact, there are two obvious ways in which any theory of art may be attacked. It might be argued that it counts too little as art, or that it counts too much. That is, it might be argued that the definition does not provide necessary conditions for something to count as a work of art, or it might be argued that it does not provide sufficient conditions. Let us consider these in turn.

V

To begin with, then, it might be held that there are works of art which the definition does not count as such, and thus that the definition does not provide a necessary condition for something to count as a work of art. One sort of case that may seem to provide difficulty in this regard is the ready-made. For here, though there is indeed an intersubjectively available product, there seems to be no artistic process whatever. Duchamp did not make *Bottle Rack*, he merely bought and displayed it. But again, I want to countenance as parts of the artistic process not merely the manipulation of materials, but the whole mental and physical series of events by which a work is made intersubjectively available. Whether ready-mades count as works of art depends upon the sort of process by which they came to be displayed. If Duchamp regarded the mental exercise of conceptualizing and displaying ready-mades as satisfying for its own sake, then they are works of art. Thumbing one's nose at the art world is certainly admissible as an artistic purpose, and the question then becomes whether any particular thumbing of the nose is the product of an artistic process. To try to decide *that* question, one must make an historical investigation. Furthermore, *Bottle Rack* has a place in certain human activities, particularly museum-going. If it is of a kind which can make such activities themselves absorbing (and if it is in fact the product of an artistic process), then it is a work of art.

However, there is another argument that suggests that absorption in process cannot yield a necessary condition for something to count as a work of art. It might be asserted that much of what currently appears in museums and stages and concert halls just is not produced by processes pursued for their own sake. For example, it might be pointed out that Warhol was notoriously indifferent to the means by which his works were produced, often refusing even to supervise their production, which in any case was carried out more or less mechanically. Now I do not know whether this is indeed a correct way to characterize Warhol's works. But it certainly is the case that not everything that is displayed and appreciated as art was produced by a process which was regarded by its creator as intrinsically worthwhile.

Nevertheless, I do not think that this fact militates against the present view. In arguing against the institutional theory, Ted Cohen has pointed out that it does not provide any conditions of failure, that on it it is impossible to try to make a work of art and fail, or to wrongly accredit something as a work of art.[11] This is indeed intuitively unsatisfying. On the present view it is perfectly possible to discover that something that has been hanging in a museum to the rapt admiration of all is not a work of art. It is perfectly possible that Warhol was not an artist but a charlatan. (I do not *assert* that Warhol was a charlatan, only that my view makes sense of the accusation.) What would be required is an examination of Warhol's creative process, a process about which there is certainly rich documentation. If we do not ourselves find in Warhol's work an enhancement of our own experience, that may, again, constitute evidence that his products are not works of art. (However, I do think Warhol's works are art, in part because I do find such enhancement in them.)

This raises yet another difficulty, however, which is bound up with the very notion of a process theory, a difficulty which we broached earlier. For a work of art does not wear the process that produced it, as it were, on its sleeve. It may in some cases be impossible to reconstruct that process, or it might even be held that because the process is in part an inner series of events in the artist's mind, it is in principle inaccessible. And this problem is especially acute when, as I will do throughout this book, we move afield from our own culture, where the psychology and spirituality may appear alien. But even if the process were inaccessible, it would not follow that it is not process that makes something a work of art. No one may ever see a quark or a lepton, but it does not follow that the disposition of quarks and leptons does not in some sense explain the disposition of medium-sized physical objects. Furthermore, often (as in the case of Warhol), there are perfectly plausible ways to go about finding out how a purported artist worked, and how he thought about how he worked. Sometimes this can be plausibly inferred merely from the work itself. That is, the character of the object may itself be evidence that it was produced by an artistic process. Anyone asserting that Titian was not devoted to and absorbed by the juxtaposition of colors, or Beethoven to and by the juxtaposition of tones, has some

explaining to do. And as for the claim that the mental processes of an artist are in principle inaccessible, this appears to
me to be simply a variety of scepticism about other minds, and
to deserve whatever treatment we may want to give that position.

Finally, it has been suggested that, for example, religious
painters of the middle ages offered their works as benedictions
to God, and perhaps even regarded their own works as called
forth by divine intervention, as, in some sense, not *their* works
at all. In fact, and as we shall see, the sense of a loss of self in a
devotional process is typical of artistic process in many parts
of the world. But I do not think that such cases, even if this is
an accurate description of them, provide genuine counter-
examples. First of all, the devotion of such painters to their
process is evident in their products, and in the apprenticeships
they served in order to be able to produce them. And we ought
to ask, as an addendum to the *bricoleur* problem, why such artists produced paintings, say, rather than merely engaging in
the forms of benediction prescribed for all worshipers. I take it
that, whether divine inspiration was in question or not, such
painters took painting itself to be a peculiarly satisfactory
offering to God and occasion of worship, and took themselves
to be peculiarly suited to provide such offerings and occasions.

It is more likely, however, that the objection to the present
theory that will immediately leap to the reader's mind is that
it counts far too much as art. Art is often distinguished from
craft, but no such distinction seems to be available on the
present view. In fact, crafts, according to my definition, are
paradigmatic arts, and I think this is a strength, rather than a
weakness, of the view. I really do not see why (some) furniture
makers, potters, blacksmiths, and ostrich-egg decorators
should not be accredited as artists. If it is asserted that this is a
mere abuse of words, I would point out that, whether from an
etymological residuum of the ancient Greek or whatever
cause, such activities are often enough in the common parlance counted as arts. One may well say admiringly of a certain blacksmith, who with evident satisfaction produces a

good horseshoe, that he is a real artist. I take such locutions seriously.

The potter Carla Needleman, in fact, describes her process in just the terms I have been setting out:

> I could go on about the study of trimming the bottom of the plate to get the foot rim, the various discoveries I made about how dry the plate has to be before it can be trimmed, where to place the rim so that the plate looks right on the table, [and so forth]. . . . But the effort of precision, the search for perfection, is not undertaken for the sake of the finished product. If I don't have a goal, an aim, how will I know when I fall short? But if I have only the goal, how will I see where I am now?[12]

Art, in this sense, is "seeing where I am now." It is becoming absorbed in what one is doing at the present moment, in the process one is engaged in right now. In this sense, art is a coming to presence within one's artistic process.

And it is just here that the normative, as opposed to descriptive, agenda of the definition is evident. For the present definition indeed counts as art a tremendous number of items that never issue into the museum, the skyline, the book of poems, the stage. So among other things, I reject the distinction between the "classificatory" and "evaluative" senses of 'work of art' introduced by Weitz and taken up by Dickie and others. According to these thinkers, to say, for example, that a cake is a work of art is simply to praise it as a good cake; it is not literally to place it in the same category as Rembrandt's self-portraits. The cake is art only in the "evaluative" and not in the "classificatory" sense. My definition tends to count as art in the "descriptive" sense what these philosophers count as art in the "evaluative" sense. In fact, the distinction between "classificatory" and "evaluative" senses appears to me to be merely a way of enshrining extremely problematic distinctions between "fine art" and the various things to which it is opposed in the philosophical and critical literature: popular art, folk art, craft. I will have much more to say against these distinctions later.

But Weitz's distinction of 'art' into various senses seems to me unmotivated and invidious in the first place. We ought to be extremely leery of multiplying "senses" of terms. At the very least, if there are both evaluative and classificatory senses, they are obviously related. 'Art' is not a homonym. Take the term 'king.' We sometimes use it to refer to the male monarch of a nation, but we also use it in several "figurative" or "evaluative" ways, as when we refer to a magnate as "The King of Pork" or a pornographer as "The King of Sleaze" or to Elvis Presley simply as "The King." I suggest that we are not dealing with separate senses, or at the least, if we are, that the "evaluative" sense is parasitic on the "classificatory." There is a range of cases for the proper use of the term 'king,' from the paradigmatic to the fanciful. Indeed, most natural language terms have such a range of application. If the extended uses were in fact different 'senses' of the term, those extended uses would be incomprehensible. That is, the extended uses receive their sense from the paradigmatic uses, and cannot be isolated from them without losing their meaning. I am, then, arguing that the paradigmatic cases of art are not limited to the museum and the concert hall. I take it that ditch digging, philosophy, or quilting can quite literally be artistic activities. Of course it is easier to find satisfaction in some processes than in others, but virtually no process is necessarily devoid of intrinsic satisfaction if it is pursued in the right spirit.

Though I reject any principled distinction between classificatory and evaluative senses, my definition does not provide a full-scale evaluative program for works of art. A very bad work of art may arise from a process that is paradigmatically artistic, and may certainly be *of a kind* (e.g., High Renaissance painting) that is suited to enhance experience. For example, I do not reject various evaluative criteria that arise from Western characterizations of art, though I reject the characterizations. Other things being equal, it is better for a work to be formally interesting than not. Furthermore, given that there is a plurality of artistic ends, it is plausible to evaluate at least some works of art by how well they serve the ends for which they are created. For example, if an altarpiece is designed to arouse the viewer to adoration, but in fact is merely ugly and commonplace, it is a bad altarpiece. Notice that its chances are considerably enhanced if it was made by an artist in devotion to the process of its making.

This will certainly raise another objection. Calling Elvis "The King" does not deploy a different sense of 'king' from the usual, but it does use the term in a metaphorical way. Metaphorically, Elvis is the monarch of rock; his fans are his "subjects." (Of course, and again *contra* Weitz and Dickie, the metaphorical use is dependent on the paradigmatic use, and does not yield a new sense of the term.) By parallel, it might be asserted that various uses of the term 'work of art' which my definition counts as literal are in fact metaphorical. If we say of a blacksmith or a quilter or an advertising designer that they are producing works of art, it will be claimed, we may be using the term metaphorically.

As the sketch of a response to this objection, it seems to me that whether a word is used figuratively or metaphorically on a given occasion is relative to the etymology of the word. The literal sense of a term, on this suggestion, is to be found by tracing its history, and looking for some core of early uses that are properly related to its present extension. We shall have a chance to look at the history of the term 'art' in somewhat more depth later. But very briefly, the word 'art' in its derivation from the Latin 'ars' and so on originally denoted great devotion and skill in a wide variety of endeavors; it picked out certain characteristics of process rather than, say, certain mediums such as painting and sculpture. Phrases such as "the art of war," "the art of cooking," "the art of love," and so forth are extremely well-established, indeed ancient, usages. By contrast, the widespread use of the term and its cognates in other languages in a specialized sense to refer to what we think of as the fine arts dates from the eighteenth century,[13] or at very earliest from the Renaissance. This suggests (though of course hardly demonstrates) that the sort of extension countenanced for 'work of art' on the present account does not merely confuse literal and metaphorical uses. It suggests, that is, that the compartmentalization of art against which Dewey and many others have inveighed corresponds to a relatively late *restriction* of the use of the term (a restriction which in turn, and as we shall see, corresponds to the beginning of the discipline of art history and of the museum system). If this is so, a definition such as the present one can claim not to be simply countenancing metaphorical usage as literal, but rather deploying a literal use of the term, and, furthermore, a use that is still in general circulation. And to relate the present proposal to the etymology of 'art,' it seems to me that when someone is pursuing an activity for its own sake, with loving absorption, that person is very likely to develop great skill in making the objects to which that activity gives rise. And objects that are skillfully made are suited to enhance the experience of those who use them.

But what is accounted art in the restricted use of the term that developed in eighteenth century—the notion of the "fine arts"—emerges out of a wider context of satisfying and absorbing activities, and this is not adventitious. It is bound up with the basic conditions of human life, and is found wherever human beings are found.

Notes

1. See, e.g., Morris Weitz's classic article "The Role of Theory in Aesthetics," *Journal of Aesthetics and Art Criticism*, 15 (1956).

2. See George Dickie, *Art and the Aesthetic: An Institutional Analysis* (Ithaca: Cornell University Press, 1974); "The New Institutional Theory of Art," in *Aesthetics: A Critical Anthology*, ed. George Dickie, Richard Sclafani, and Ronald Roblin (New York, St. Martin's Press, 2nd ed., 1989), 196–205. Jerrold Levinson, "Defining Art Historically," *The British Journal of Aesthetics* 19, 3 (Summer 1976): 232–50; "Refining Art Historically," *The Journal of Aesthetics and Art Criticism* 47, 1 (Winter 1989): 21–33.

3. Two recent books which argue this point elaborately, and which, I think, provide a wealth of empirical evidence for a theory of art such as the one put forward in this paper are Richard Anderson, *Calliope's Sisters: A Comparative Study of Philosophies of Art* (New York:

Prentice-Hall, 1990), and Ben-Ami Scharfstein, *Of Birds, Beasts, and Other Artists* (New York: NYU Press, 1989), which for my money is the best book in aesthetics to appear in many years.

4. Richard Wollheim, *Painting as an Art* (Princeton: Princeton University Press, 1987), especially chapter 1.

5. John Dewey, *Art as Experience* (New York: Minton, Balch & Company, 1934).

6. Audrey Flack, *Art and Soul* (New York: E. P. Dutton, 1986), 10.

7. Dewey, *Experience and Nature* (New York: Dover, 2nd ed., 1958), 361.

8. Wollheim, *Art and Its Objects* (Cambridge: Cambridge University Press, 1980), section 22 et seq.

9. See, e.g., Dewey, *Experience and Nature* (New York: Dover, 1958), chapter 3.

10. Horace Kallen, *Art and Freedom* (New York: Duell, Sloan, and Pearce, 1942), 950, 51.

11. Ted Cohen, "A Critique of the Institutional Theory of Art: the Possibility of Art," reprinted in *Aesthetics: A Critical Anthology*, 1st edition, ed. George Dickie and R.J. Sclafani (New York: St. Martin's Press, 1977), 192.

12. Carla Needleman, *The Work of Craft* (New York: Arkana, 1986), 17, 18.

13. The first such use recorded in the *Oxford English Dictionary* dates from 1680.

Chapter 2

Zen and the The Art of Living

If the sort of view that I have just put forward is right, then art is a way of leading a meaningful life. Many of us have pursued a goal single-mindedly, only to find that, when it is achieved, we have a feeling of emptiness. One reason for this is that we focus exclusively on the goal and regard the means of achieving it merely as obstructions. It is thus possible to become miserable while realizing our most cherished desires. But if the process by which such desires are realized is itself absorbing, the time expended in their realization has not been wasted. I take seriously and literally the claim that a person's life may be a work of art, that there is an "art of living."

I

We might, taking the thing at its widest sweep, think of our entire lives as a single artistic process. I may have a goal in life, or I may not. Likely, I have several goals (I would like to be successful and authentic, say, as a philosopher and as a father, and so forth). But I cannot simply wish these goals to completion; they are the sort of goals that one must devote many years to achieving. Now it might be possible simply to try to rush through these years, simply to pass through them on the way to the goal, to experience them as an ordeal that must be endured for the sake of the goal. One odd thing, however, is that one is unlikely to achieve such goals if that is the way they are regarded. To become a good father: that is not something that I could, say, learn how to do by practicing, reading books, undergoing therapy and so forth, and then suddenly, as it were momentarily, be a good father. To be a good father is precisely to be present in the process of fathering, to be present to one's children as father. There is an art of fathering, but not an achievable goal of being a good father that could be described outside of that art. If I want to be a good philosopher, to take another example, I cannot simply will flawless books into existence; I must nurture my work as best I can day by day as a teacher and as a learner. Again, that is not something I could do once and for all, but something to which I must devote myself inside the moment in which I am.

Too much of our activity is mechanical, is performed with little awareness and little appreciation for process. We of the west tend to order our lives as a series of tasks, and we tend to define those tasks by their goals. We make a list of things to do in the morning, and we are satisfied (if you want to call this satisfaction) if we complete the tasks on the list. The list does not include *how* we want to achieve these goals. I don't say, "go to grocery store in deep awareness and gratitude"; I just say "go to grocery store." But it has to be precisely in the mundane activities of our everyday lives that we come to awareness, if we come to awareness at all, because almost all of our lives consist of such activities. Very few of us have the luxury, or for that matter the inclination, to devote our lives to a spiritual path by, say, joining a monastery. But we do not need to be monks if we can dig our ditches, mow our lawns, shop for our groceries, or care for our children with devotion, with the feeling that these activities can be consecrated. Such activities may not yield works of art. But they can be experienced as artistic activities when they are experienced in devotion to process.

The practice of coming to awareness, or mindfulness, in the ordinary activities of life is central to Zen Buddhism. A Zen monk chops wood, cooks, cleans, and so forth not only to maintain himself and his fellows, but as a spiritual discipline. The Zen master Thich Nhat Han describes the process of washing the dishes as follows:

While washing the dishes one should only be washing the dishes, which means that while washing the dishes one should be completely aware of the fact that one is washing the dishes. At first glance, that might seem a little silly: why put so much stress on a simple thing? But that's precisely the point. The fact that I am standing there and washing these bowls is a wondrous reality. I'm being completely myself, following my breath, conscious of my presence, and conscious of my thoughts and actions. . . . If while washing dishes, we think only of the cup of tea that awaits us, thus hurrying to get the dishes out of the way as if they were a nuisance . . . we are not alive during the time we are washing the dishes. . . . If we can't wash the dishes, the chances are we won't be able to drink our tea either. While drinking the cup of tea, we will only be thinking of other things, barely aware of the cup in our hands. Thus we are sucked away into the future—and we are incapable of actually living one minute of life.[1]

People often seek peace and enlightenment by intense spiritual discipline, or travelling to exotic places, or in fevers of penitence. The odd thing is that enlightenment is found exactly where we already are; enlightenment consists in opening up to and affirming the situation we are already in. All the shit that I have to do every day may seem to me to be the barrier to my peace; in truth, the things I do every day constitute the only place in which I could possibly find my peace. And if I am going to open myself to what I already have and what I already am and what I already do, if I am going to live artfully, then I had better start with the real things I do every day, things like washing the dishes. If I defer my peace until I meet my goals, I will find no peace when I get there. That is what Thich Nhat Han means when he says that if I am incapable of washing the dishes mindfully because I am looking forward to tea, I will not be able to drink my tea mindfully either. The art of living is, thus, an art of the most mundane, modest (and, thus, also truest) moments in our lives.

Thomas Alexander, in his excellent discussion of Dewey's aesthetics, connects it with Zen. Central to Dewey's view, Alexander argues, is the notion of "living in the present as process."[2] He continues:

> One is connected to the world in the living moment. To be so totally integrated in the moment is just what the Zen Buddhists call "enlightenment." It is simply "being-*there*"—that instant of complete awareness in which subject and object disappear, in which one doesn't so much see the Buddha as become him.

Thus, in Zen, mindfulness and devotion to process are connected with a fusion to the divine: one's fusion to a world in process, and to the things with which one works within that world is itself the content of religious devotion. This is a structure that I think is typical in the arts of the world, and to which I shall return in chapter 6: the fusion with materials that is the basis of art enables and is the occasion of wider fusions: with other persons, with and within a culture, and with the gods.

Tantrism, or Vajrayana, is another form of Buddhism (and, for that matter Hinduism), which affirms life in process, which calls us to an awareness of what we are already doing. The Buddhist nun Pema Chödrön defines Vajrayana as "the practice of taking the result as the path."[3] This would mean, for example, taking *nirvāna* to be this world, or taking our current ignorance as complete enlightenment. Our ignorance would then consist in failing to realize that we were *already* enlightened. Pema Chödrön's teacher, Chögyam Trungpa, writes:

> In tantra, it is necessary to have pride that we are taking a journey; it does not really matter whether it is a forward or a backward journey. A journey is actually taking place—that is what counts. . . . When we refer to a journey, it seems to be quite clear that we are not talking about struggle or ambition. On the other hand, maybe we *are* talking about struggle and ambition: ambition in the sense that we are inspired into the nowness, this very moment, and struggle in that a

sense of exertion or discipline in the practice is necessary.[4]

Art as a mode of living, in other words, demands real exertion
and discipline, and real desire for goals. But it demands, above
all, immersion in the journey itself: in some sense the path is
itself the goal. *That we are on the way* is both the most obvious
fact about us and the key to bringing ourselves into awareness
of reality.

Art and craft is both a central metaphor and a central
example of what it is to come to presence or mindfulness in
one's life. As such, it is central to what I have been calling spirituality, and it is hardly surprising that artistic activities lie at
the heart of all the world's spiritual traditions. As Carla
Needleman says with regard to her life and craft:

> I need to be where I am. When I'm not, when I'm lost
> somewhere out there, I am alienated from my life and
> all my thoughts and feelings take place in dreams—
> whether pleasant or unpleasant dreams doesn't mat-
> ter. Simply put, if my life is to have meaning, I need to
> be alive inside my own skin. Craft is a way of working
> to be alive inside my skin.[5]

This has the trivial ring of the most profound truths. "I need to
be where I am": the need to be where one is is a need that cannot but be satisfied; I always already am where I am; it is not
as though I need to *get* someplace to be where I am already.
But that is precisely the point. Art is a way of experiencing the
truth, of coming into what is already the case. It is not reality
that needs alteration, or on which we work through art; it is
our own illusions.

II

I would now like to develop what I regard as a central illustration of the theory of art and of the art of living that I have been
putting forward: the Japanese tea ceremony. The tea ceremony, as the name implies, is a ritual in which tea is con-

sumed; it is a ritual way of preparing and drinking tea. Now drinking tea is part of everyday life; in fact, it's something most Japanese folks do most days. Raising such an activity to the realm of art thus has a particular resonance. People spend lifetimes learning and performing the tea ceremony. And this, I think, confirms what I am saying about art: it is a *way* of doing whatever it is you do: it is a *tao*, the *tao* of tea. Indeed, the tea ceremony is called in Japanese *chadō*: the way of tea. The tea ceremony raises life to the level of art by focusing on an everyday activity with tremendous concentration and performing it for its own sake. The tea ceremony seeks transcendence through immanence; it makes an art of life. And it is not surpirising that it is bound up with Zen.

"Simply make fire, boil water, and drink tea," wrote Nambō Sōkei, a sixteenth-century tea master. "The tea ceremony is nothing other than that."[6] And, stripped to the essentials, the tea ceremony is indeed just the everyday activity of tea. However, to emphasize the *art* in the ceremony, to encourage the participant to focus with intensity on the mundane activity, the classical tea ceremony is hedged around with incredibly detailed ritual prescriptions. These prescriptions govern the approaches to and arrangements within the tea room, the items used to prepare and serve tea, the order and character of the actions performed, and the content of conversation during the ceremony. Oddly enough, however (and this is connected with the origins of the tea ceremony in Zen, Taoism, and Confucianism), the tea ceremony is also supposed to have an absolutely spontaneous and even informal quality.

Now think about that for a moment. One is supposed to perform the ritually prescribed actions in the ritually prescribed way, and one is supposed to do so spontaneously. It immediately becomes apparent that that is a task which could absorb a whole life. And in fact many lives have been spent in the way of tea. One must cultivate the rituals so assiduously and at such a deep level that they become wholly internalized; when one asks oneself what one most wants to do *right now*, the answer has to be the particular ritually prescribed action of, say, turning the tea cup two quarter-turns. One performs the action freely, easily, and naturally, and yet one performs it in an exactly specified manner.

Jorge Luis Borges, in a story that has entered the literature of aesthetics through the work of Arthur Danto, describes an author, Pierre Menard, who, in the early twentieth century, wrote part of *Don Quixote*. This was not a new version of *Don Quixote*, nor an adaptation of Cervantes. Rather it *was* Cervantes' *Quixote*, word for word. Nevertheless, despite its formal identity to Cervantes' work, Borges asserts that Menard's *Quixote* is stunningly different than the original. For example, he says, "the archaic style of Menard . . . suffers from a certain affectation. Not so that of his precursor, who handles easily the ordinary Spanish of his time."[7] At any rate, it took Menard roughly a lifetime to complete a few chapters of his book. That was because he used a very interesting technique. In Menard's own words: "My solitary game is governed by two polar laws. The first permits me to attempt variants [on Cervantes] of a formal and psychological nature; the second obliges me to sacrifice them to the 'original' text and irrefutably to rationalize this annihilation" (p. 51). In other words, he had to come up with decisive reasons why *each word* of Cervantes has to be precisely what it is. That is, roughly, also the aesthetic structure of the tea ceremony; what is apparently a mechanical process has a subterranean existence as an immense act of simultaneous self-affirmation and self-annihilation. One sacrifices oneself to the ritual by an inexorable logic.

But the case of the tea ceremony is even harder than the case of Menard's *Quixote*. For after one sees that no variation could possibly count as an improvement, the proper actions now have to emerge spontaneously. It is as if Menard just found himself *wanting*, on his own, to set down the exact words of Cervantes. It is this that gives the tea ceremony a totally absorbing character; it is a very simple ceremony—minimalist in its aesthetic—but one that can be entered into at any level of depth of which the participant is capable. Of course, such simultaneous rigidity and spontaneity may be impossible, but that also helps make it worthy of pursuit. And this aspect of the tea ceremony is supposed to reverberate into the entire experience of the tea master; since he is performing a mundane activity, he is learning to perform mundane activities in a beautiful, ritualized, and spontaneous way.

The tea room is in a sense set aside from the everyday. It is quiet, purified of business, its very size (typically four and a half mats, or nine feet square) ritually prescribed and set apart. But it is more accurate to describe the enclosure as synecdoche of the everyday. The everyday is brought into the tea room in a ritually prescribed way. The tea ceremony is *not* a perfection of the everyday world. In fact, as Kakuzo Okakura puts it in *The Book of Tea*, the tea ceremony "is essentially a worship of the Imperfect, as it is a tender attempt to accomplish something possible in this impossible thing we know as life."[8] The tea room is supposed to be scrupulously clean (this is, possibly, an element derived from Shinto rites of purification). Again, one might think of this as a way of distinguishing the tea room from everyday life, though it provides an opportunity to perform the mundane act of cleaning mindfully. But consider this story of the tea master Rikyū, retold by Okakura:

> Rikyū was watching his son Sho-an as he swept and watered the garden path. "Not clean enough," said Rikyū, when Sho-an had finished his task, and bade him try again. After a weary hour the son turned to Rikyū: "Father, there is nothing more to be done. The steps have been washed for the third time, the stone lanterns and the trees are well sprinkled with water, moss and lichens are shining with a fresh verdure; not a twig, not a leaf have I left on the ground." "Young fool," chided the tea-master, "that is not the way a garden path should be swept." Saying this, Rikyū stepped into the garden, shook a tree and scattered over the garden gold and crimson leaves, scraps of the brocade of autumn! What Rikyū demanded was not cleanliness alone, but the beautiful and natural also. (pp. 36, 37)

Similarly, all trace of symmetry is avoided in the room itself and its accessories; one would rarely use a perfectly matched set of dishes, for example. In fact, the implements are often selected to create an aesthetic of *wabi*, or poverty. Yasuhiko Murai describes that aesthetic as follows:

> Rikyū's achievement represents the culmination of the *wabi* aesthetic born of the contemplative awareness of the relationship between people and things. While cha-noyu [tea ceremony] necessarily involved the element of material things . . . the *wabi* ideal originated in the idea of negation or lack. In the first anthology of Japanese poetry, the eighth-century *Man'yø-shū*, *wabi* meant simply poverty or meanness.[9]

Murai describes the development of the notion into a positive aesthetic in the poetry of Saigyø (1118–90) and Shinkei (1406–74), among others, and then quotes a poem by Fujiwara Ietaka (115–1237), said to be one of Rikyū's favorites:

> Show them who wait
> Only for flowers
> There in the mountain villages:
> Grass peeks through the snow,
> And with it, spring.

The beauty of *wabi* is the beauty of the everyday, not the exceptional. It is the beauty of the typical, of the things that go unnoticed until we learn to approach them mindfully. And the tea ceremony is precisely a context in which this mindfulness can be cultivated, in which the everyday is isolated, in its everyday-ness, for appreciation.

Often, rough and flawed pots and cups are employed, and many of these items are justly famous, not as perfect exemplars of the potter's art, but as perfect images of the imperfect in human life. Ueda retells a story of Rikyū:

> One day Rikyū and Joo, another great sixteenth-century tea master under whom Rikyū himself studied tea as a youth, were invited to a tea ceremony together with a couple of others. On the way to the host's residence they saw a vase for sale. Joo liked it very much, but as he had company he said nothing at the time and sent for it the next morning. To his disappointment, he

found the vase had already been sold. Then an invitation to tea came from Rikyū, who said he would like to show a vase he had just bought. Joo went, now realizing that Rikyū was the one who had beaten him to the vase. Indeed there the vase was, with two camellia flowers neatly arranged in it, but, strangely enough, one of ears of the vase had been broken off. While other guests sat wondering, Joo said to Rikyū: "It is strange that you have chipped an ear off that vase. From the moment I saw the vase yesterday, I have been fascinated by it and kept thinking that I would use it at my tea ceremony, but only after breaking off an ear. So, before I came here this morning I had planned to carry out a scheme. Thinking that it wouldn't be very interesting to chip off an ear after discussing the matter with you at the end of the ceremony, I had planned to break off an ear myself at the recess or some such time." So saying, Joo took out a hammer from his pocket. (91, 2)

The tea implements are imperfect precisely because the tea ceremony is not an attempt to escape or evade the imperfection of life through art, but an attempt to affirm life in all its imperfection. In "worshipping the imperfect" one learns to live artistically outside the tea room. Some of the implements designed and used by Rikyū are still extant. If one looks at such famous tea bowls as the "Great Black" or the "White Heron," for example, one sees that they are absolutely simple in design, and absolutely rough in execution. They possess the character of natural, unworked material; they are true to the world in the sense that they are true to the materials out of which they are constructed. And they are affirmations of the world in the sense that they are occasions for finding the greatest beauty in the simplest stuff of reality.[10]

In an alcove called the *tokonoma* within the tea room, there is usually a flower arrangement (along with a hanging scroll of calligraphy or representational painting). This flower arrangement, too, is often an affirmation of life in its imperfection, rather than an idealization. One major school of flower arranging (which is, like the tea ceremony itself, an art form to which one can devote a lifetime) is the naturalistic school. One should not, on this view, employ flowers that are out of season, for example. In the winter, one might even display bare branches (a further expression of *wabi*). And one is to arrange the flowers and branches in a way compatible with the ways flowers and branches actually grow. For example, the branches should not extend below the level of the top of the vase, which represents the ground. Water may be scattered over the blossoms and the vase, giving the cooling quality of dew. And nature is brought into the tea ceremony in other ways: the tea room is often approached by a "garden path" through a naturalistic garden, as we have seen. And the temperature of the tea and the quantity served may be adjusted to the weather, in order to satisfy thirsty guests on a hot day, or warm them up on a cold one.

One feature that is immediately noticeable about the tea ceremony is that it integrates many arts. One approaches the tea room through a carefully landscaped garden. The tea room itself is often a masterpiece of simple architecture, and the carpenters who build them are often venerated. The tea room encloses the potter's wares, often decorated with sculptural details or lacquered. The kettle is sometimes filled with iron pieces to create a jingling music. Flower arranging and painting or calligraphy are often incorporated. The ritually prescribed movements have the character of a dance, and the ritually prescribed speeches (inquiring about the origin of the implements, for example) the character of drama. This very integration intensifies the aesthetic experience: it is the creation of a total environment that is meant to be completely absorbing. The circumstances are designed to create an aesthetic situation, not of distance or disinterest, but of engagement. (Arnold Berleant has argued eloquently that that is a feature of the experience of the truest art.[11]) What one does in the tea room one does for its own sake, and for the sake of giving everyday life an aesthetic character.

It is often asked whether we should think of the tea ceremony as a religious rite, a social occasion, or a work of art. The ceremony indeed derives from ceremonies performed in Zen monastaries, and, as I have said, also displays Taoist, Shinto, and Confucian elements. (The very respect for tradition that it incorporates is a Confucian aspect, bordering on ancestor-worship.) And the tea ceremony is beyond doubt a social occasion. Among other things, it has the effect of breaking down the social barriers within a hierarchical society. All of the guests typically enter through a low door, so they are all equally forced to bow upon entering. One is not supposed to talk politics. Instead, one talks freely and spontaneously (in the ritually prescribed manner!) about the utensils, the weather, and so forth. The participants are to be treated as equals, and though one guest is typically singled out as honored, this is not always the one of the highest social standing, and those of higher social standing must still pay their respects. And the tea ceremony, as we have seen, is obviously a multimedia artistic extravaganza (albeit a minimalist one). So which is it?

Fortunately, the present theory of art allows us to give no answer to this question, whereas several of the traditional Western theories might force us to. The tea ceremony has social and religious purposes, social and religious content. But that is obviously not incompatible with it being a work of art. Whatever the purposes for which the tea ceremony is performed, it is also performed for its own sake; it is elaborately designed to be intrinsically absorbing: all of its elements conspire to that effect. So on my view it is a paradigm of art. And since it is precisely an art of life, an art of eating and drinking and talking and loving nature and other human beings, it encapsulates the basic point of this book: that between life and art no decision is necessary, that we can live our art, that life and art are intimately connected and at their best moments identical.

I would like to conclude this chapter by quoting a passage from Okakura which I think is, roughly, the most profound thing I have ever read:

The Taoists relate that at the great beginning of No-Beginning, Spirit and Matter met in mortal combat. At last the Yellow Emperor, the Son of Heaven, triumphed over Shuhyung, the demon of darkness and earth. The Titan, in his death agony, struck his head against the solar vault and shivered the blue dome of jade into fragments. The stars lost their nests, the moon wandered aimlessly among the wild chasms of the night. In despair the Yellow Emperor sought far and wide for the repairer of the Heavens. He had not to search in vain. Out of the Eastern sea rose a queen, the divine Niuka, horn-crowned and dragon-tailed, resplendent in her armour of fire. She welded the five-coloured rainbow in her magic cauldron and rebuilt the Chinese sky. But it is also told that Niuka forgot to fill two tiny crevices in the blue firmament. Thus began the dualism of love—two souls rolling through space and never at rest until they join together to complete the universe. Everyone has to build anew his sky of hope and peace.

The heaven of modern humanity is indeed shattered in the Cyclopean struggle for wealth and power. The world is groping in the shadow of egotism and vulgarity. Knowledge is bought through a bad conscience, benevolence practiced for the sake of utility. The East and West, like two dragons tossed in a sea of ferment, in vain strive to regain the jewel of life. We need a Niuka again to repair the grand devastation; we await the great Avatar. Meanwhile, let us have a sip of tea. (8,9)

Yes, let's. Art brings with it the potential of social and cosmological transformation. But it is a transformation that renounces the *effort* for transformation; it is a transformation achieved *here and now* by focusing on what we are now doing, not as a means of transformation, or not only as such a means, but also for its own sake. Kierkegaard once said that the most difficult task is "to strive to become what one already is." He asks: "who would take the pains to waste his time on such a task, involving the greatest imaginable degree of resignation? Quite so. But for this very reason alone it is a very difficult task, the most difficult of all tasks in fact, precisely because every human being has a strong natural bent and passion to become something more and different."[12] Art is a means of focusing on what we already are, and thus transforming ourselves. It is a way of appreciating what we already have, becoming absorbed into what is already there. The tea ceremony encapsulates this process.

Notes

1. Thich Nhat Han, *The Miracle of Mindfulness* (Boston: Beacon Press, 1987), 3–5.

2. Thomas Alexander, *John Dewey's Theory of Art, Experience, and Nature: The Horizons of Feeling* (Albany: State University of New York Press, 1987), 195.

3. Pema Chödrön, *The Wisdom of No Escape* (Boston: Shambhala, 1991), 9n.

4. Chögyam Trungpa, *Journey Without Goal* (Boston, Shambhala, 1985), 119, 120.

5. *The Work of Craft*, 32, 33.

6. Quoted in Makato Ueda, *Literary and Art Theories in Japan* (Cleveland: The Press of Western Reserve University, 1967), 95.

7. Jorge Luis Borges, "Pierre Menard, Author of the *Quixote*," trans. Anthony Bonner, in *Ficciones*, ed. Anthony Kerrigan (New York: Grove Press, 1962), 53.

8. Kakuzo Okakura, *The Book of Tea* (New York: Dover, 1964), 1.

9. Yasuhiko Murai, "A Brief History of Tea in Japan," in *Chanoyu: The Urasenke Tradition of Tea*, ed. Søshitsu Sen, trans. Alfred Birnbaum (Tokyo: John Weatherhill Inc., 1988), 22.

10. For illustrations of these bowls, see Hayashiya Seizo, *Chanoyu: Japanese Tea Ceremony* (Tokyo: Japan Society, 1979), 162, 163.

11. Arnold Berleant, *Art and Engagement* (Philadelphia: Temple University Press, 1991).

12. Søren Kierkegaard, *Concluding Unscientific Postscript*, trans. David F. Swenson and Walter Lowrie (Princeton: Princeton University Press, 1974), 116.

Chapter 3

Art and War: Paradox of the *Bhagavad-Gītā*

The "art of living" in the sense developed above is the central theme of the great classic of Hinduism: the *Bhagavad-Gītā*. The first several chapters of the *Gītā* set themselves a daunting task: to explain how a life of action can be rendered compatible with a life of renunciation of desire. The situation, in fact, is designed to raise the issue in an excruciatingly intense form. At the climax of the epic known as he *Mahābhārata*, Kṛṣṇa—an incarnation of the Supreme Lord—and Arjuna—the war leader of the heroic Pāṇḍavas—pause on the verge of the decisive battle. Arjuna asks how killing his enemies, who include his own teachers and members of his family, in order to secure power and fame, can be squared with his religious and ethical convictions. In this chapter I will try to explicate Kṛṣṇa's solution of the paradox, not from the point of view of Hindu tradition (in which it has driven whole movements of thought), but from the point of view of the notion of the art of living as it has been developed so far. I will wind up arguing that the paradox of the *Gītā* suggests a reconstrual of the way we conceive the relation of means and ends in our activities, a reconstrual that can be profitably understood through the concept of art. And I will argue that this reconstrual has the potential to change our relations to our world and to one another in a way that is deeply life-affirming.

I

Let us begin by setting the familiar scene. The battle between the massive armies of the Pāṇḍavas and the Kauravas, who are related by history and ties of blood, is about to be joined. As Arjuna rides out in his chariot to survey the field, he loses his desire to fight, despite the fact that he is the bravest of men. He expresses his misgivings to his charioteer Kṛṣṇa, an incarnation of the Supreme Lord.

Verses I:28–36 broach the theme that to kill, much less to kill one's own teachers and one's own kin, in order to achieve worldly power, seems to be a direct violation of the traditional religious and ethical constraints of which Kṛṣṇa is in some sense himself the author: "I do not long for victory, O Kṛṣṇa, nor kingdom nor pleasures. Of what use is kingdom to us, O Kṛṣṇa, or enjoyment or even life? . . . Only sin will accrue to us if we kill these criminals."[1] This is, indeed, a major theme of the *Mahābhārata* as a whole: the suspension of the ethical in the enactment of fate. Certainly, the actions themselves which Arjuna is contemplating—fratricide and so forth—are monstrous, though their ignominy may be mitigated somewhat by their occurrence in the context of war, and by the history of the relations between the two branches of the Kurus. As he says at I:43, by this war, "the immemorial laws of the race and the family are destroyed." But as the *Gītā* continues, it appears that Arjuna also has misgivings at an even deeper level. The ends for which the war is being prosecuted by the Pāṇḍavas, and even the sheer fact that it is being prosecuted for ends at all, appear problematic in relation to the Vedic teaching of which the teachings of the *Gītā* itself are an elaboration.

One would not, it seems to Arjuna, engage in action at all, much less furious, horrific action of the sort he is contemplating, if one were not moved by desire (for power, revenge, and the like). The war into which he is about to enter is undertaken as a sheer means to these ends (obviously not, for example, because he thinks killing members of one's own family, or being killed by them, is intrinsically pleasurable). But this appears to violate the entire deportment with regard to the world that is prescribed in the Vedic tradition. In that tradition, desire (which is always desire for some end), and passion (the attitude in which one finds oneself as one furiously attempts to realize the object of desire), are, apparently at any

rate, barriers to liberation (*mokṣa*). One is to seek nonattachment to things of this world, and in particular to the sorts of
things Arjuna stands to gain by victory. (Early Buddhism and
Jainism were particularly committed to nonattachment, and
perhaps Kṛṣṇa's reply can also be regarded as a reply to these
views.) Thus Arjuna says, at I:45, 46: "Alas, what a great sin
have we resolved to commit in striving to slay our own people
through our greed for the pleasures of the kingdom! Far better
would it be for me if the sons of Dhṛtarāṣtra, with weapons in
hand, should slay me in the battle, while I remain unresisting
and unarmed." And finally, at II:9, Arjuna resolves not to
fight.

Now Kṛṣṇa tries several approaches to convince Arjuna
that he ought to attack, and it is possible to interpret them,
first, as inconsistent with one another, and second, as apparently disingenuous attempts at persuasion rather than as sin-
cere arguments. I will come back to these later, in order to consider the second claim, but the first seems obviously
compelling. At II:11–25, Kṛṣṇa argues that death is an illusion,
that "Of the non-existent there is no coming to be; of the exis-
tent there is no ceasing to be" (II:16). Immediately following
that, however, at II:26–30, Kṛṣṇa claims that death is inevita-
ble, and that "for what is unavoidable thou shouldst not
grieve" (II:27). These apparently incompatible passages are
followed by a section in which Kṛṣṇa rather superficially
exhorts Arjuna to do his duty and discharge his obligations,
whereas it might be pointed out that Arjuna is already at loose
ends precisely about where his duty lies, and to whom he is
obliged. Now I think some of these apparent tensions can be
resolved, but this resolution will emerge only at a later stage
of the discussion.

After running through these arguments, Kṛṣṇa (at II:47–
53) proceeds to formulate what many have regarded as the
central message of the *Gītā*, as well as the point at which it
departs from, or at a minimum elaborates in a fundamentally
new direction, traditional teachings: "To action alone hast
thou a right and never at all to its fruit; let not the fruits of
action be thy motive; neither let there be in thee any attach-

ment to inaction." And he adds: "When thine intelligence, which is bewildered by the Vedic texts, shall stand unshaken and stable in spirit (*samādhi*), then shalt thou attain to insight (*yoga*)." This last sentence allows us to see that Kṛṣṇa is explicitly considering and dismissing the claim that to engage in this war is to violate Vedic ethics, and he appears to be cautioning Arjuna not to take the Vedic texts too literally.

Now the very familiarity of Kṛṣṇa's basic claim—that one should act, but renounce one's right to the fruits of one's action—can blind us to its deeply paradoxical nature. To put it at its most stark: Why would a person who was not motivated by desire for certain results act at all? It seems that all human action is for the sake of some end. If one renounces desire for the object of one's actions, if one is not intent on achieving something and acting in the belief that one could, through one's actions, attain the object of desire, one would, it seems, never begin. When one asks: Why did someone do *that*, rather than *this*?, one is often asking about the ends that person had in view. And as one *selects* the actions one takes, one does so, normally at any rate, by reference to the conduciveness of various courses of action to the ends one desires to achieve. If one renounces the fruits of action, it seems, one might as well renounce action completely.

In fact, the circumstances of the *Gītā* seem especially designed to raise this paradox in its most extreme form. Killing, and risking being killed, are things that it seems *no one* in his right mind would do, unless he believed that some great purpose was to be achieved by doing so. War is the most obvious case in which, as we say, if the means can be justified at all, they can only be justified by the ends in view. Kṛṣṇa demands of Arjuna the following apparently impossible task: act so as to attempt to achieve, by means Arjuna himself regards as horrific and sinful, a certain set of ends, while simultaneously letting go of those very ends. That is, he asks Arjuna to act, immediately and irrevocably, while at the same time removing all normal motivation to act. That is the paradox of the *Gītā*.

II

Arjuna, then, and we, insofar as we are people of action rather than pure contemplation, seem to be in a situation in which we ought to act, but in which the normal motivations for action, and ways to deliberate between actions, are unavailable. Nor do we have the option of simply failing to act. As Kṛṣṇa points out (III:5), "no one can remain even for a moment without doing work; everyone is made to act helplessly by the impulses born of nature." To renounce all action, to engage in asceticism after the fashion, say, of the Jains, is itself to act; to cease acting by force of will is precisely to desire some end, and to act in its service. Now we might take the approach of acknowledging that what Kṛṣṇa suggests is a mystical discipline, that our task is simply to accept the paradox as a paradox, and to live with and in it. The task, thus construed, would be to put the practical rationality which we are all the time employing constantly into question.

But I do not think that such a response is in keeping with the spirit of the *Gītā*. In these passages, it seems that Kṛṣṇa is formulating a practical guide to action. Arjuna is, after all, not a mystic, but a man of action *par excellence*. And he is faced, right at this moment, with a moral dilemma which he must, immediately, adjudicate one way or the other; the armies are arrayed against one another; the fight is about to begin. Thus, I think it is legitimate, at least conditionally, to ask whether and how the paradox can be mitigated, whether there is, after all, some principle on which Arjuna can decide whether and how to act. And insofar as Arjuna is an exemplary man of action, and his situation an exemplary dilemma, it is legitimate to ask how *we* ought to act, or on what principles we choose to act (if it is indeed we who choose our actions).

Here is the solution that I think Kṛṣṇa suggests: it is not that we act wholly and always without ends; that *would* make human action impossible. Rather, we ought to reconstrue the *relation* of means to ends in our actions. We must acknowledge, first, that whereas it may be in our power to perform some action, the results of that action are not, or at any rate are not always, under our control. Arjuna can decide to attack, but he cannot decide to win. So our actions should not be performed *merely* for the sake of the end; the end must not absorb or expunge the means in our deliberation. Often, in deliberation, as I discussed in the last chapter, we *extinguish* the means in favor of the end; we regard the means merely as barriers to the realization of the end. If we could achieve the end by sheer force of will, if we could realize it without performing the means, we would. Kṛṣṇa asks us not to renounce all desire, and thus all action, but to desire the means as intrinsically valuable *as well as* valuable in the service of the end. The means are not to be absorbed in the end; the time and energy devoted to the means are not wasted. Rather, this time and energy are to be *consecrated*.

That is the view which Kṛṣṇa sets out at III:8–14:

> Do thou thine allotted work, for action is better than inaction; even the maintenance of thy physical life cannot be effected without action. Save work done as and for a sacrifice, this world is in bondage to work. Therefore, O son of Kuntī (Arjuna), do thy work as a sacrifice, becoming free of all attachment. In ancient days the Lord of creatures created men along with sacrifice, and said, "By this shall ye bring forth and this shall be unto you that which will yield the milk of your desires."

This is an incomprehensible passage if the point is simply that one is always to act with no end in view whatever. For Kṛṣṇa says that this mode of activity will "yield the milk of your desires." (A more literal translation might be: "this will be the cow that grants your wishes.") It would be ironic indeed to recommend the absolute renunciation of ends in order to achieve those very ends, to recommend the cessation of desire as a technique for realizing the objects of desire. (I will, however, explore this possibility more thoroughly in chapter 7.) Once renounced, of course, this realization could no longer motivate action.

What is suggested in this passage, rather, is that there is a *way* of working—*karma yoga*—which liberates, a way which does not entail the renunciation of ends. Rather, it demands *a consecration of means.* Work done for the sake of ends alone is "bondage." In such work, we are enslaved to the means, which we do not desire but which we must perform or endure, as we pursue the end, the object of desire. But work done in a sacrificial stance, instrumental activity that is consecrated to the Lord of Creatures, is a liberation from bondage. To put it in terms that Thich Nhat Hanh might supply: one might live a life devoted to the acquisition of power, wealth, pleasure, and so forth. In such a life, the entire activity which leads to these ends is in a sense wasted; it is neither desired nor experienced for its own sake. One wants to *get through it* as quickly as possible. If one devotes one's life to achieving such ends, one has wasted one's life up to the moment the end is achieved. If one succeeds, one has been absent from one's life up to that point, at which time one must furiously begin the task of *preserving* that which has been achieved. That is, save for, possibly, a single culminating moment, one's life has been empty of content. On the other hand, if one *fails* to achieve such ends—and whether one succeeds is not, or is not only, under one's own power—one's life is entirely bathetic. One has not been *present* in one's life at all, but has lived in devotion to a moment that has never arrived.

If, on the other hand, one lives a life in which one consecrates the means, performs the means as a sacrifice, with their own meaning and spiritual content, then one has indeed been present. If one then achieves, or receives, "the milk of one's desires," one will no doubt be pleased, and one will be in a position fully to experience this culmination. But if this culmination never arrives, one's life has been anything but wasted. At each moment, one offered one's actions in a consecration; one was present throughout. In *that* sense, one has "let go of the fruits"; it is not in achieving or failing to achieve those ends that one finds one deepest meaning, but in *trying* to achieve those ends *in the right way.*

At III:22–25, Krsna puts it like this:

> There is not for me, O Pārtha (Arjuna) any work in the
> three worlds which has to be done or anything to be
> obtained which has not been obtained; yet I am
> engaged in work. . . . As the unlearned act from attach-
> ment to their work, so should the learned also act, O
> Bhārata (Arjuna), but without any attachment, with
> the desire to maintain the world-order.

Again, this displays the apparent vacillation between the rec-
ommendation of nonattachment and the affirmation of desire,
or at least of some desires, that makes it appear obviously
inconsistent. But again, I think this inconsistency *is* only
apparent. What it means to Kṛṣṇa to consecrate one's actions,
to perform them in a spirit of sacrifice, is to perform them in a
way that "maintains the world-order." That is, one acts as a
part of the greater whole, in the experience of being situated
within the order of things. Kṛṣṇa's model for this, not surprisingly given the last two chapters, is of a humble laborer or arti-
san, who is devoted to his work, rather than to its fruits.

In one sense, indeed, it is not the individual who acts at all;
the world-order acts *through* the individual. "He who sees that
all actions are done only by Nature (*prakṛti*), and likewise that
the self is not the doer—he verily sees" (XIII:29). So when one
acts in a consecration of means, one ceases, in some sense, to
be the *agent* of one's actions; one acts as a part of the world-
order. Or better: one loses the *illusion* that one is the agent of
one's actions; one comes to see one's actions as *prakṛti* acting in
and through one's body. (I will develop this suggestion much
more elaborately later.)

This culminates Kṛṣṇa's solution of the paradox, and I
think that it supplies a clear answer to the problem, though
one which it is unutterably difficult to apply in one's life. The
task that Kṛṣṇa presents to us is a task to absorb an entire lifetime.

It is the task of learning to make and drink tea.

III

Now I would like to explore the extent to which we can understand this solution and apply it if the full-fledged context of belief in which it emerges is in some sense unavailable to us. The Vedic sacrificial practices and the detailed cosmology of the later parts of the *Gītā* itself are not live options for *me*, a Westerner who lacks religious commitment. There is no question, at the moment, of my consecrating my actions to Kr̥ṣṇa, for example. Nevertheless, the reconstrual of the relation of means to ends found in the *Gītā* is something I feel both the need for and the possibility of in my own life. Specifically, I want to understand Kr̥ṣṇa's solution of the paradox with reference to *art* (*śilpa*), which, to repeat, I take precisely as a form of human instrumental action that exceeds *mere* instrumentality, in which means are not expunged in ends.

Art is a mode of activity in which the means of arriving at the end maintain their integrity in the face of the end. This is not, as we have seen, to say that art is pursued without any end whatever; indeed, it is perfectly possible to seek wealth or fame or sexual conquest by making art. (Art has undeniably been made for these purposes.) Nevertheless, the *means* by which these goals are pursued, from the initial emotional impulsion or idea that generates a work, to the activity of manipulating materials, or tones, or words, that yields the finished work, are also engaged in for their own sake. And the products thus produced are themselves suited to play a role in such activities. As we have begun to see, the absorption in materials that is achieved in art is the first moment of absorption into the world; to make a work of art is in this way to allow nature or the world to act through one's body.

I think it is clear that, in this use of the term, art is human activity that approaches the ideal set out in the *Gītā*. That is, I would like to identify *karma yoga* and *śilpa-karma* (artwork). In the *Gītā*, three ways of achieving liberation are described: *jñāna yoga* (the way of knowledge), *bhakti yoga* (the way of devotion), and *karma yoga* (the way of action).[2] Art, in this sense, is the way of working that liberates, in particular that liberates in devotion to means from slavery to desire (though not from desire itself).

Art is, in secular terms, a way of accounting for what, in religious terms, Kṛṣṇa characterizes as the performance of each action as a sacrifice. Art consecrates its activities and its objects, and as art becomes a way of life, it consecrates each human action by focusing on it for its own sake. One *devotes* oneself to each action as one performs it. And art, at its height, yields a sense that one is no longer the sole agent of one's own action. A potter of my acquaintance says that his best work is accompanied by the sensation that *he* is not making the pot, but that the pot is using his hands to take shape. That is the sense that the Greeks associated with poetic rapture, with being possessed by the muses.

IV

The situation of the *Gītā* is designed to emphasize relentlessly the fact that *any* human activity can be undertaken as an art in this sense. That is because it takes place on the verge of war. Kṛṣṇa exhorts Arjuna to fight, and to fight as an art, to fight and to consecrate his fighting, to fight for the sake of fighting, and for the sake of fighting beautifully. Many cultures, including Western culture, have regarded war as an art in this sense. But obviously, killing and dying are extremely difficult to engage in for their own sakes, and it might well seem to be morally abhorrent to do so. And it *would* be impossible to engage in war as an art if one's moral principles made it absolutely impossible to regard killing as an activity in which one could potentially be engaged for its own sake. I do not mean to minimize the deep moral problems that arise when killing is regarded as an art, or the deep religious problems that arise when killing is regarded as a sacrament. But in this light, Kṛṣṇa's initial exhortations to Arjuna, to the effect that killing destroys nothing, and that everyone dies anyway, and that fighting is Arjuna's moral duty, become comprehensible. They are precisely ways of trying to show that the activities are *not* so morally and religiously appalling that they cannot be engaged in as an art.

It is clear enough, in fact, that in many cultures fighting a war *can* be pursued for its own sake. In the novel *Little Big Man*, Thomas Berger puts the following words, which are profoundly in keeping with the philosophy of life of the Native Americans he is describing, in the mouth of a chief of the Cheyenne, Old Lodge Skins, who is speaking after the battle of Little Big Horn:

> [W]hite men, who live in straight lines and squares, do not believe as I do. . . . They will even fight at night or in bad weather. But they hate fighting itself. Winning is all they care about. . . . [K]illing is part of living, but they hate life. They hate war. In the old days they tried to make peace between us and the Crow and Pawnee, and we all shook hands and did not fight for awhile, but it made everybody sick and our women began to be insolent and we could not wear our fine clothes if we were at peace. So finally we rode to a Crow camp and I made a speech there. "We used to like you when we hated you," I told those Crow. "Now that we are friends of yours, we dislike you a great deal."
>
> "That does not make sense," they said.
>
> "Well, it wasn't our idea."
>
> They said: "Nor ours. We used to think you Cheyenne were pretty when we fought you. Now you look like ugly dogs."
>
> So it was an emergency and we had a great battle.[3]

War, Old Lodge Skins is saying, can be a necessary and beautiful thing, despite its horrors, and war can be life-affirming because killing and dying are part of life. As Kṛṣṇa puts it: "to the one that is born death is certain. . . . [F]or what is unavoidable thou shouldst not grieve" (II:27). The Cheyenne fought as a celebration of life, as Kṛṣṇa urges Arjuna to fight. For the Cheyenne and for Arjuna, winning is not the only point, though they fight to win. They have ends in view, but they live and die in the means.

Now the major theme of the *Mahābhārata* is what Kierkegaard called "the suspension of the ethical." In the course of the battle that follows the *Gītā*, each of the Pāndavas violates their dearest moral principle. For example, Yudhisthira, who is the embodiment of truth, tells a lie in order to defeat his own beloved teacher. Each of the transgressions is urged precisely by Krsna, each is necessary to achieve victory, and, finally, each is represented by Krsna as fated. In this way, the Pāndavas, as they proceed through the story, learn humility in the face of destiny, whereas a too-great virtue is represented as a resistance to fate and to God, that is, as pride. Finally, they achieve fusion with the divine precisely in a transgression of divine law.

Obviously, the full-fledged ethical impact of the *Gītā* cannot be reproduced in a secular context. But here is an interpretation: transgression of moral principles in a devotion to a world in process is an acknowledgment of evil, an allowance of the world to be, with its evil as well as its good; likewise, it is an allowance of oneself to be, without moral expurgation of the self. It is an attempt to identify oneself, through devotion to process, with a cosmic order which is itself indifferent to good and evil, a universe that has no moral content, or at any rate is not clearly or wholly good. In that sense, transgression becomes sacrament, becomes affirmation of the real.

I will develop this thought at great length elsewhere. But for now, I want to acknowledge, first, that it is a dangerous, indeed an abysmal thought. But I think it is also a deeply affirmative thought, a thought that leads us, finally, into a love for the world and for one another. For if we do not acknowledge the evil in what we love—in our fighting, in our culture, in our lovers—then it is not truly they whom we love. We can become fused, artfully fused, with evil persons, evil movements, wars, and so forth, and we are properly subject to moral disapprobation when we are. But even, or perhaps especially in that case, we are also affirming our world, and ourselves as beings in that world.

V

It is obvious, I suppose, that on this view of human acting, human making, and art, the distinction between beauty and use breaks down. The beauty of an item to be produced might well be the end for which it is produced, but one lives within the means of arriving at the end; the process is the use of beauty, or the emergence of beauty from use. Beauty in this sense is bound up with process; it is, in particular, the suitedness of the product for use; its suitedness to enhance intrinsically whatever use it has. Thus, the distinctions between beauty and use, fine and applied art, art and craft, structure and ornament, all break down in a picture of human activity such as that put forward in the *Gītā*. All of these features are discussed in an exemplary way by Ananda Coomaraswamy, whose aesthetics emerges self-consciously from the Indian tradition as embodied in *Gītā* and in traditional Indian art.

Coomaraswamy writes:

> [The] distinction of pure or fine art from applied or decorative art, and of beauty from use, has been drawn in Europe only within the last two centuries [Coomaraswamy is writing in 1937], before which time the terms "artist" and "artisan" designated only the professional maker, without regard to the kind of thing made. The new distinction belongs to the ideology of industrialism, seeming to explain and justify a division of craftsmen into artists on the one hand and laborers on the other. ... Actually there never has been, and never can be agreement as to the point at which art ends and industry begins; the categories as defined being always opinionative and without authority.[4]

I will return the question of the relation of art to industry in the last chapter of this book, in a discussion of Taoism and Heidegger. But for now I want to call attention to the organic connection between beauty and use that Coomaraswamy identifies in non-European and earlier European art.

In fact, Coomaraswamy, drawing on a venerable tradition, identifies beauty with adaptation to use:

> [A] well-made sword is not more beautiful than a well-made scalpel, though one is used to slay, the other to heal. Works of art are only good or bad, beautiful or ugly in themselves, to the extent that they are or are not well and truly made (*sukṛta*), that is, do or do not express, or do or do not serve their purpose. (75)

In the discussion above of the process definition of art, I spoke of the enhancement of experience pursuant to the use of objects that are "well and truly made," that are made in a devotion to process. But "enhancement" is in some sense a misleading or impoverished term. It suggests that there is some substrate of sheer utility on which is overlaid an aesthetic surface that yields pleasure. But in an exemplary work of art, a work of beauty in Coomaraswamy's sense, there are not two separable moments: the moment of use and the moment of appreciation of decoration. The activity of use is instead permeated by the beauty of the object; the entire character of the activity is shaped by the beauty of the object. To use a sword that is well-balanced, perfectly sharpened, and has a grip that fits beautifully in the hand is to fight in a different way and with different results than to fight with a sword made (so to speak) by a hack.

A central term in Navajo aesthetic and spiritual life is *hózhó*, the primary meaning of which is beauty. But *hózhó* also means practical utility and moral goodness. Finally, it means a kind of universal harmony; a harmony of and in the universe as a whole. Here, the aesthetic appraisal of something as beautiful is simultaneously the appraisal of it as good after its kind, and as right within the cosmos.[5]

On the other hand, in the Western tradition, as Coomaraswamy very rightly points out, the notion of ornament or decoration has come to mean something superfluous to function, something added for the purpose of sheer visual pleasure. We think of ornament not as something necessary to the proper functioning of the functional items we employ, but as pleasant (or perhaps simply useless, or luxurious) accretions applied to the surface. Coomaraswamy traces the etymology of words in Indo-European languages that are used for adornment, ornament, or decoration, and reaches these conclusions:

> It will be found that most of these words, which imply for us the notion of something adventitious or luxurious, added to utilities but not essential to their efficacy, originally implied a completion or fulfillment of the artifact or other object in question; that to "decorate" an object or person originally meant to endow the object or person with its or his "necessary accidents," with a view to proper operation; and that the aesthetic senses of the words are secondary to their practical connotation: whatever was originally necessary to the completion of anything, and thus proper to it, naturally giving pleasure to the user. (242)

"Aesthetic" ornament, in this sense, may be pleasurable, but the pleasures it yields are superficial in relation to the person who has them, just as the ornaments themselves are superficial in relation to the armature of the utilitarian item onto which they are grafted. The ornament does not engage the item; and the very same decorative motifs could be applied at will to different sorts of things: clothing, say, and wallpaper. And the pleasure that is yielded does not engage the person; it does not emerge out of and in the activities in which the person is engaged. It is a mere play of shape and color: "formal" and "aesthetic" in that sense, and to that extent ephemeral and superficial. But an ornament that alters and interpenetrates the full-fledged human activity yields a pleasure that runs deep and which endures as long as the activity endures. Ornament in this sense is *hózhó*; it is beautiful *in virtue* of its enhancement of the activities for which it is designed.

One particularly clear example of this is in literature, in which beauty as adaptation to use has not wholly dissipated. Now there *are* aesthetic novels, poems, plays, and so forth:

works in which the sprightly play of verbal form is the source of whatever pleasure the work is capable of yielding. But there are many other works in which the form and content cannot be separated, in which beauty is use. Think, for example, of the novels of William Faulkner. It would be absurd to say, for example, that we could have *the very same stories* in another prose style, that Faulkner's style is in an aesthetic sense an ornament of the plot, and so forth. Rather, Faulkner's stories can *only* be told in the voice he tells them; the sense of intensity, of overflow, of loss of control are intrinsic to the substance. There is no distinction between style and substance, form and matter, process and product. It is predominantly in the visual arts where these things have come apart, to their unspeakable impoverishment, and ours. Coomaraswamy writes:

> The exact measure of our indifference to [real] values is reflected in the current distinction of fine and decorative art, it being required that the first shall have no use, the second no meaning: and in our equivalent distinction of the inspired artist or genius from the trained workman. We have convinced ourselves that art is too good a thing for this world, labor too brutal an activity to be mentioned in the same breath with art; that the artist is one not much less than a prophet, the workman not much more than an animal. Thus a perverted idealism and an amazing insensibility exist side by side; neither condition could, in fact, exist without the other. All that we need insist upon here is that none of these categories can be recognized in Asia. (126)

The sentence I would like to pluck from this admirable paragraph is the claim that we regard art as something too good for this world. I think that is a profound commentary on Western art of the twentieth century.

Precisely in pursuit of art for art's sake, or art which does not contain a meaning outside itself, formal or aesthetic art, modernism progressed as a movement into abstraction. This progress, I assert, can be understood as a retreat from the real, an expression of fear and hatred of the world. (Of course, it is not without good reason that people fear and hate the world!) This art often understood itself as the construction of alternate realities or the discovery and expression of realities that already existed, for example, "spiritual" realities of the kind invented or located and subsequently painted by early abstractionists such as the "medium" Hilma af Klimt or Kandinsky. Modernism sought detachment first of all from the social context, and also from the physical context, of the real, whether it was into a realm of pure spirit or a realm of pure form (both of these, to be sure, are fictional realms). In the next chapter, these developments will be explored at greater length.

If we could return to a sense of the artistry and dignity of labor, to the usefulness of beauty, and to the immanence of the spiritual in the physical world, we could restore ourselves to reality. The *Gītā* does not tell us to stop acting, or to engage in different actions than we are engaged in right now. It tells us to consecrate the actions we are currently performing, and to perform them in awareness of their place in the world. Whereas Western art has attempted to attack or flee from the real, much Indian art—both Asian and North American—calls us to a consecration of ourselves to the real. We of the west have tried to make a useless beauty; but no true beauty is without a use.

Notes

1. *The Bhagavad-Gītā*, trans. S. Radhakrishnan, in *A Sourcebook in Indian Philosophy* (Princeton: Princeton University Press, 1957). All quotations are from Radhakrishnan's translation.

2. See Radhakrishnan's introduction to the *Gītā* in *A Sourcebook of Indian Philosophy*, 102.

3. Thomas Berger, *Little Big Man* (New York: Dell, 1964),441, 442.

4. Ananda Coomaraswamy, "The Part of Art in Indian Life," *Traditional Art and Symbolism* (Princeton: Bollingen, 1977), 73n.

5. See Gary Witherspoon, *Language and Art in the Navajo Universe* (Ann Arbor: The University of Michigan Press, 1977), chapter 4.

Part Two

Aesthetic Reintegration

It is by now obvious that I believe that the most problematic aspect of the fine arts in Western culture is their estrangement from everyday life. My proposed characterization of art is both descriptive and normative. It is an attempt not only to capture what works of art have importantly in common, but to retrain our sights on a wider set of objects and activities than we are accustomed to think of as art. It is both a theory of art and a plea for what we might call aesthetic integration: a way of showing the artfulness of living: the life in art and the art in life. Whereas the first part of this book focused on the descriptive project, I would now like to turn to the normative.

I will start with a brief description of aesthetic estrangement, the process by which Western artists have become ever more intensely conscious of themselves as artists and ever more intent on exclusion, and I will proceed to describe some strategies for experiencing ourselves and our culture as artistic. I will focus at length on blues and country music as, first, things many of us experience every day and, second, ways of displaying and recovering the legitimacy of our traditions and rituals. I will discuss, as well, the possibility of a full integration of art into education. Finally, I will discuss the arts of our culture in relation to the problem of technology.

Chapter 4

The Future of Art

Arthur Danto, in his infamous essay "The End of Art," contends that the history of art is the history of the development of a certain sort of self-consciousness, that art has itself been the attempt to discover the nature of art:

> Art is a transitional stage in the coming of a certain sort of knowledge. The question then is what sort of cognition this can be, and the answer, disappointing as it must sound at first, is the knowledge of what art is. . . . [T]here is an internal connection between the nature and the history of art. History [on Hegel's view] ends with the advent of self-consciousness, or better, self-knowledge. I suppose in a way our personal histories have that structure, or at least our educational histories do, in that they end with maturity, where maturity is understood as knowing—and accepting—what or even who we are. Art ends with the advent of its own philosophy.[1]

Various facts bear this out, at least to a certain extent and in a certain way. Avant-garde artists through the nineteenth and twentieth century seem to have cultivated a consciousness of themselves as artists, and of the place of their products within the unfolding of art history, that displays an ever-increasing intensity.

Now self-knowledge and self-consciousness are to some degree desirable, as much of the history of philosophy has been devoted to establishing. But too much self-consciousness is madness. It is possible to suffer from a surfeit of self, a surfeit in which, paradoxically enough, the self may be pulverized. Excessive self-consciousness can lead to a need for oblivion, an impulse toward self-destruction.

Danto claims that art ends when it becomes its own philosophy, when it discovers its own nature. This makes the concept of art something that is either extremely profound or extremely paltry. For notice that the nature of art, on this view, is that art is the discovery of its own nature. So what we discover when we discover the nature of art is that art is the very discovery we are now having. Art is the discovery of itself, which is the discovery of itself, and so forth. This in a certain sense denies that the concept of art has any content whatever; its content is the discovery of itself, the nature of which is in turn itself, that is, its own discovery. Art is then not an arena of human endeavor or a range of objects, but a structure of consciousness, a structure reflecting infinitely back on itself like the image of a mirror in a mirror. What is reflected is . . . a reflection.

Now I am not sure what value such a structure of consciousness might have; I have a tendency, manifested above, to diagnose it as a certain sort of neurosis rather to celebrate it as an interesting human achievement. But art in *that* sense, Danto claims, is now finished, because art *has* discovered its own nature (or at least, philosophers have discovered it in art); art has discovered that it is its own discovery.

Now it seems to me that the story Danto tells of the history of art, the narrative that culminates in the moment of discovery of discovery, is true, more or less. But I will argue that it is true only of a certain very small segment of the entire historical and geographical range of the arts: namely, the Western avant-garde arts of the last two hundred and fifty years or so. And I will argue that the fact that this development culminates in art's discovery of itself as its discovery of itself shows that there is something empty (and perhaps pathological) about the concept of avant-garde art. Further, I want to try to reconstrue parts of this history, not only as the attempt to discover what (avant-garde) art is, but also as the attempt, through that discovery, to destroy (avant-garde) art. That is, hidden in the will to self-knowledge, or perhaps motivating that will, is the will to self-destruction. In this way, we could articulate the teleology of twentieth-century avant-garde art as a movement simultaneously toward the discovery and destruction of itself. Fortunately or unfortunately, that movement has, it seems to me, been an abject failure: every increase in self-consciousness has just made art's sense of its own existence more indefatigable; ironically enough, the will to self-destruction is what has sustained and what still sustains avant-garde art. Finally, I will go on to suggest how art could be reintegrated into the life of our culture. Or rather, I will suggest that it has never ceased to be so integrated.

I

Perhaps the clearest crystallization of the sort of self-consciousness we are discussing is the phrase 'art for art's sake,' or *l'art pour l'art*. Here again we face the possibility of a regress which is either empty or profound. The purpose of art is itself, which is its own purpose, and so forth. The phrase as it developed is one of the key and characteristic moments of modernity. The phrase has its origins in French romanticism, and conveys the idea that art should not be evaluated moralistically or religiously, that there is an autonomous and incommensurable realm of aesthetic value. In this sense it in part represents the romantic attack on neo-classicism, which insisted above all on "content" of a moral/historical variety. At its most extreme, the doctrine of art for art's sake holds that art is of no *use* whatever, that it has no real-world application, and is the appropriate object of an absolutely "pure" regard. The notion has been fundamental both to the liberation of the imagination that is associated with romanticism, and to the creation of the avant-garde. But the ideology it represents has also been at the heart of the deeply problematic nature of modernism and the twentieth-century avant-garde's attempts at self-destruction.

In an interesting discussion of the origin of the phrases, John Wilcox traces it, rather comically, to a garbled and incompetent reading of Kant's aesthetics by French intellectuals of the early nineteenth century.[2] It is generally agreed that the first use of the phrase in something like its present sense occurs in the diaries of Benjamin Constant in the year 1804. Constant was a French journalist who visited Weimar in the winter of 1803–04, where he frequented the circle of Goethe, Schiller, and Schelling. In his diary he wrote: "I have a visit with Robinson, pupil of Schelling's. His work on the *Esthetics* of Kant has some very forceful ideas. *L'art pour l'art* without purpose, for all purpose perverts art."[3] To say that this is a simplified version of Kant is an understatement. Nevertheless, the notion that art should be made and appreciated for the sake of art alone has its origins in Kantian disinterestedness. This is true also of its use by the incompetent interpreter and brilliant teacher Victor Cousin, who taught a course in aesthetics at the Sorbonne in 1818. The course was eclectic, but focused on (roughly) Kantian notions of free beauty and the independence of artistic from religious, moral, and practical value. Cousin's course was highly influential on the next generation of French thinkers including Jouffroy, and, through him, Sainte-Beuve.

These were, however, only intermittent outbreaks, though they expressed the emerging romantic sensibility toward the aesthetic. The phrase entered general circulation in France in 1834 with the publication of Théophile Gautier's *Mademoiselle de Maupin*. In the preface, he wrote that "Only those things that are altogether useless can be truly beautiful; anything that is useful is ugly, for it is the expression of some need, and the needs of man are base and disgusting."[4] (This strikes the note of self-loathing that in some sense persists throughout the history of the avant-garde.) The phrase and the sensibility it embodied (often termed "aestheticism") were taken up by such figures as Flaubert, Baudelaire, and Mallarmé. A particularly clear statement of the view is provided by Flaubert's correspondence with George Sand, in which Flaubert asserts against Sand the claims that art need not be morally uplifting, that beauty is opposed to utility, that style can be distinguished from content, and so forth.[5]

The view was taken up, as well, by British aesthetes, most famously by Oscar Wilde and Walter Pater. Pater, for instance, argued passionately that human wisdom is found in the immediate enjoyment of experiences for their own sake, rather than in the conceptual reconstruction of experience. Here are the famous final lines of Pater's *The Renaissance* of 1868, for instance: "Of such wisdom, the poetic passion, the desire of beauty, the love of art for its own sake, has most. For art comes to you proposing frankly to give nothing but the highest quality to your moments as they pass, and simply for those moments' sake."[6] From this it is clear that "art for art's sake" was used both as a theory of how, or at any rate why, art was to be created, and a theory of how art was to be regarded. It was to be created for "purely aesthetic" reasons, and evaluated without recourse to moral, religious, or practical standards.

Among the consequences of art for art's sake as a mode of regarding art is the claim that art is not to be appreciated for what might be termed its anecdotal value, its value as a representation. This is in part because the representation of human action or even of natural scenery always seems to possess a moral or religious dimension. Even the still life and landscape of seventeenth-century Holland, for instance, have been read as elaborate religious allegories. This in turn suggests (a notion that appears, albeit qualifiedly, in Kant), that the aesthetic properties of a work of art, the properties that are relevant to an experience and assessment of it *qua* art, are the formal properties: the arrangement of lines and colors, rhythms and tones, masses and curves. Pater's account surely suggests, in fact, though Pater himself drew this implication only inconsistently, that the representational content of a work is at best of secondary value. For the point in Pater is the immediacy of a sense experience: the value that is yielded on an analysis of representational content, or what we can see through the work to, is not "immediately" experienced in this sense.

This move into aesthetic immediacy, so beautifully captured in Pater's prose, had massive implications for the history of art and thought about art in the West. In art history, it led directly to the development of elaborate formal analysis of the sort most famously exemplified by Heinrich Wölfflin's *Principles of Art History*. In painting, it resulted in the development, first, of ever-greater representative distortion in the work of the late impressionists and post-impressionists, and finally, in the second decade of this century, in the development of pure abstraction. In literary theory, the New Criticism of pure text and the intentional fallacy developed from this base. In aesthetics, the result was the virulent formalism of such figures as Clive Bell, Roger Fry, and, to some extent, Clement Greenberg. Bell, for example, wrote that "to appreciate a work of art we need bring with us nothing from life, no knowledge of its ideas and affairs, no familiarity with its emotions."[7] And here is Greenberg:

> It has been in search of the absolute that the avant-garde has arrived at 'abstract' or 'non-objective' art. . . . The avant-garde poet or artist tries in effect to imitate God by creating something valid solely on its own terms . . . something *given*, increate, independent of meanings, similars or originals. Content is to dissolved so completely into form that the work of art cannot be reduced . . . to anything not itself.[8]

The avant-garde art world of this century has persistently attempted to put the ideology of art for art's sake into operation, and the ideology persists. In 1993, for example, the abstract painter Ellsworth Kelly wrote, regarding a blockbuster Matisse exhibition at the Museum of Modern Art: "Personally, I believe in *art for art's sake* and I believe Matisse did also. He only painted to please himself, not to please the world, nor to change the world."[9]

In one way or another, then, the notion of art for art's sake has deeply informed Western art for one hundred and fifty years. The avant-garde constructed and then deconstructed itself within this notion. It is worth holding on to some of the original motivations for the notion. For example, there can be more to art than sheer didacticism or edification. The demand that art be pedagogical or edifying was rightly felt as an arbitrary restraint by the romantics, and the notion of art for art's sake played its part in a liberation from philistinism. There is truth, as well, in Pater's connection of art to a devotion to the present, and to presence, though, as we have seen, such devotion does not demand purposelessness. On the other hand, the notion itself is highly problematic. We know enough to be suspicious at this point of the claims of *any* human endeavor to escape the exigencies of class, politics, morals, and so forth: even the withdrawal from the political is a political act. Certainly, Bell's claim that to understand art we need bring with us nothing from life is baldly ridiculous. We always do bring with us something from life, and if we were able jettison life completely we could understand nothing whatever.

So the view is implausible in its most extreme forms. But what is more relevant here is the structure of consciousness it embodies. Artists come, in the history we have been tracing, more and more intently to regard themselves *as* artists. As Greenberg wrote and recommended, they literally separate themselves from the culture as a whole in the pursuit of their activity. But the activity becomes a rather odd and involuted one in that it is its own purpose, or, on Danto's terms, its purpose becomes the discovery of itself. At first this is experienced as, and really is, a liberation. But subsequently it gets caught up into a structure of intensifying self-consciousness that comes to be intolerable.

II

Now the realm of art for art's sake, the province of the avant-garde, represents, by the standards of the theory of art developed earlier, only a tiny proportion of the arts of Western culture. And thus Danto's thesis, that art is at an end, though it might even be true of the sort of art with which he is concerned, is not true of most of the art of Western culture. And it is certainly not true of the art of non-Western cultures, to most of which the notion of art for art's sake is alien. Here is a range of items: Mahalia Jackson's rendition of "If I Can Help Somebody," Russian icons, Yoruba festival masks, Navajo sand-paintings, the Japanese tea ceremony, the Taj Mahal. Now I assert that these are all examples of art, though Danto might well deny that the term 'art' is properly applied to these items. Of course the term 'art' *is* applied to such items all the time; indeed, in some sense things such as these are central cases of art, as the term is used in the vernacular. Danto, in fact, uses the term 'art' to mean Western fine arts of the last three hundred years or so. Now it is wrong to say that any of the items listed above is *about* art, though it is pretty easy, in each case, to say what the work *is* about. Mahalia's song is about helping people: that is what it explores, and it would be strange, to say the least, to say that it was in any sense about the nature of art, though it is right here being used in a discussion of that nature. Nevertheless, Mahalia Jackson is one of the great artists of the twentieth century. Russian icons are about the content of Christianity, and not, for example, a sophisticated commentary on how that content can be depicted in art. The Japanese tea ceremony, as we have seen, is about the distillation of experience and the celebration of imperfection, and though it represents a profound form of self-consciousness, it is not a consciousness of itself as art that gives the ceremony its content.

Danto's thesis holds, if it holds, only for the "fine" arts; it does not hold for the useful arts, the decorative arts, the popular arts, or the industrial arts. Further, the thesis holds only for the secular fine arts of Europe and European-oriented cultures, and only for the period from the eighteenth century to the present. This follows, indeed, from the fact that the fine arts as we now conceive them were only distinguished from these other sorts of art from that time forward. The emergence of this notion of the fine arts coincides with the emergence of the philosophy of art and the history of art as these are currently understood. It turns in part on the very notion upon which Danto's thesis rests: that art makes progress, that art can be understood teleologically. This claim, indeed, generalizes from the descriptive to the normative; the claim that art makes progress, a claim which makes possible the construction of art history as a narrative, becomes an imperative: progress is necessary; progress is desirable; the good artists are those who make progress; the good artists are the original artists; the good artists are those who attack or destroy the tradition. ("We are primitives of a new, completely transformed sensibility."[10]) And though Vasari, say, constructed a narrative of art history, he, like his contemporaries, was immune from the astounding claim that the past must be destroyed. (The claim is astounding for at least two reasons. First, the past has already been destroyed, in virtue of the fact that it is past. But second, the past cannot be evaded as informing the present, and least of all is it evaded when its rejection is a primary motivation. Either way, the past cannot be destroyed.)

Thus was generated the familiar romantic myth of the artist as an isolated genius, emerging from his garret just long enough to astound the world with his literally stunning works. This is the way the life of Beethoven, for example, has been reconstructed, and perhaps it was in part the way the life of Beethoven was lived. (Compare this, e.g., to the life of Handel.) Or again, think of the lives of the great romantic poets: geniuses tortured in and by the pursuit of their art: fatal, unconventional, sexy. The realists and impressionists enacted the same role in the realm of painting. And the role grew in scope and in intensity: the suicide of Van Gogh, the misunderstood genius whose works could only be grasped by the future; the emigration of Gauguin, who had to return to the savage to purify himself of bourgeois conventions; the slow pickling of Jackson Pollock's liver, held hostage to the superhuman demands of revolutionary inspiration.

To repeat, the demand was always for *formal* originality, for the production of shapes that had never been produced before. Thus art became more and more purged of content; it fled not only the tradition and the bourgeoisie, but finally from the world. Art was to be purified of the mundane, whether this was understood as a physical simulacrum of pure spirituality, as in Kandinsky, or simply as a manipulation of form without reference (Kenneth Noland, for example, or Morris Louis), or as a turning away from the outer to the inner terrain, as in the expressionists. Art thus sought self-referentiality: it appeared to transcend the social, the objective, and the historical.

Now whether any person could possibly transcend these things is, I suppose, an open question. But either way, it is not self-evident that it would be desirable to transcend these things even if it were possible. A human being who is cut off from the external world, including the world of social interaction and cultural tradition, is alienated. There is a certain charm in alienation, especially when it is adopted as a pose and expresses itself in black turtlenecks, berets, hallucinogens, and bongo drums. But actually to *be* alienated in this way is an all-day sucker. It is not easy to live cut off from people, and even from nature, with only one's own monstrously bloated pretensions for company. And indeed, the romantic suffering artist is only too readily parodied, especially at the point where he begins selling very well. Genius is a burden, especially when it is a self-consciously adopted pose.

I think that much of the history of modern art has arisen from the backlash against this picture of the artist and of art. On one level, real alienation begins to be experienced as intolerable, as something that stands in need of therapy. On another level, the egomaniacal artist dressed in black becomes a worthy subject for ridicule; the pretensions of art become themselves subjects for art (a factor which reflects and contributes to the ever-intensifying sense of self-consciousness). Much of the philosophy of art of this century has been devoted to attacking what Dewey calls the "compartmentalized" conception of art, and Gadamer calls "aesthetic differentiation."[11] What they reject is the alienation of art into the province of an elite, and its removal from the day-to-day life of the culture. This alienation is signified by the literal isolation of esteemed works of art in special institutions such as museums. The works of art are gathered up and deposited behind marble walls in a physical enactment of aesthetic distance or disinterest.

And not only much of the philosophy of art, but much of the art itself of this century has been devoted to ridiculing or destroying aesthetic differentiation by ridiculing the museum-system, the art market, the history of art, or the notions of disinterestedness or distance. Let us consider a few examples, several of which, understandably, provide key moments in Danto's teleology. Consider, then, Duchamp's ready-mades. They are comprehensible as an effort to bring art back into life, to collapse the distinction, in Danto's terms, between works of art and mere real things. We could understand this either as an ontological apotheosis for bottle racks, urinals, and so forth, or as a demonstration that, after all, statues are just stones, paintings just paint. Either way, the ready-mades bring art and life back together precisely within the context in which their (supposed) distinction has reached its greatest breadth: the high modernist art show.

The slogan "art into life" was the rallying-cry of the Russian avant-garde of the early communist era. Great artists (Malevich, Rodchenko, and others) attempted to bring their art out of the galleries (which were at any rate by and large destroyed) and into the day-to-day life of the culture by designing Soviet propaganda materials and packaging for the goods produced by government enterprises. Ironically and appropriately enough, the authorities eventually perceived this as a danger and repressed it.

Or consider the development of pop art. Artists such as Warhol and Lichtenstein, with consummate self-consciousness, brought the "debased" images of popular culture—Elvis, Marilyn, romance comics—into the museum. This was an attempt, among other things, to ridicule the pretensions of fine art, to show us that there was already art all around us at movie houses, newsstands, and so forth. In an exquisite demonstration of this thesis by reversal, Lichtenstein eventually rehashed the history of the avant-garde as a comic book, constructing Monets and Picassos out of benday dots. In particular, he parodied the abstract expressionist celebration of the painterly gesture by producing a series of huge cartoon brushstrokes. These paintings are beautiful, hilarious, and devastating.

Oddly enough, however, the history of abstract art itself can be understood in part as an attempt to reconcile or identify art and life. Recall Greenberg: "The avant-garde poet or artist tries in effect to imitate God by creating something valid solely on its own terms, in the way nature itself is valid, in the way a landscape—not its picture, is aesthetically valid." Now on one level, this is simply romantic avant-garde rhetoric raised to the level of a religious conviction, but on another, it reflects one of the predominant themes in the development of abstract painting: the notion that the journey from representation to abstraction was the journey from the status of the work of art as a reflection of reality to the status of the work of art as itself a real thing. The ontological denigration of art (which we might express by inverting Danto's formula: real things and mere works of art) has, after all, been a theme in Western philosophy since Plato. What compromises the ontological prestige of the work of art is its status as an *image*, as a (distorted, disorienting) *reflection* of the real. That is one of the features that alienates art from life: the alleged fact that art stands from life at a distance of reflection. Thus, if art no longer yielded images of the real, it would become real; instead of reflecting the world, works of art could take their place in the realm of real things. In this sense, the development of abstraction was like the ready-made in reverse; Duchamp tried to make real things into works of art; Mondrian, say, tried to make works of art into real things.

All of these developments (and of course that's just the tip of the iceberg: consider guerilla theater, happenings, Cage's "found" music, various postmodern appropriations from mass media and popular culture, the display at the 1993 Whitney Biennial of the Rodney King beating video, etc., etc.) could be understood as attempts on the part of the avant-garde to eradicate itself. Again, a surfeit of self-consciousness can be experienced as unbearable, as something that must be discharged in order to create the possibility of self-forgetting. At least as insistently as the avant-garde sequesters itself in artists' ghettoes in New York, at least as insistently as it sneers at the mass media and the masses who like it, the avant-garde seeks to lose itself in the culture as a whole. The deepest prayer and deepest fear of the alienated genius is that she be made an average person, that she be allowed to enjoy a football game or rid her furniture of yellow wax buildup just like other folks.

She enacts this prayer and fear by displacing it into the avant-garde context, by making a bottle of furniture polish into a Work of Art.

Oddly enough, however, this does not make her art any more palatable or relevant to those who *use* furniture polish to eliminate yellow wax buildup. It renders the art utterly suspicious; it makes the polisher think (if she thinks about it) that art is a con game. Self-consciousness cannot be overcome by an act of will. Every *effort* to overcome self-consciousness only intensifies self-consciousness. When Warhol or the Whitney attempt to merge into the culture as a whole, they only succeed in intensifying their alienation from it. To put this into the most mundane possible terms: every effort by avant-garde artists from Duchamp to Barbara Kruger to merge art and life has been effortlessly co-opted by the institutions of avant-garde art, institutions which thrive on the alienated self-consciousness that is reflected most intensely in its attempt to destroy itself.

This is why, unfortunately, art in the avant-garde sense is not over at all. Though Danto is surely right to see in the history of avant-garde art an ever-increasing self-consciousness, and though he is right to find a culmination of that movement in the attempts of avant-garde artists such as Duchamp and Warhol to merge art and life, or art culture and the wider culture, he is wrong that this history is at an end. Avant-garde culture is stronger and more pretentious than ever; it continues to exist precisely in virtue of its continuing and intensifying efforts to destroy itself (though I admit that this is getting pretty boring).

III

The "differentiated" concept of art emerged from a much more general sense of 'art' as skilled and devoted human making, a sense which I have been trying to recapture as relevant to our situation today. And though the differentiated conception is peculiar to the West since the eighteenth century, skilled making is valued in all the cultures and epochs of which I am aware. It is not hard to understand why skilled and devoted making should be a more or less universal value. First of all, the products made with skill are simply better adapted to the uses to which they are put, and they are more satisfying to use for those purposes. Skill, in a variety of circumstances, can mean the difference between subsistence and starvation, or between prosperity and subsistence. Furthermore, to develop a craft skill and to employ it are, often, inherently satisfying; they yield a consciousness both of an increasing power over things and of an increasing harmony with them, a sense both of the ability to make things happen and the ability to participate in the becoming of things.

The restriction of the term 'art' to things that are made for the sake of art, or to things which appear in galleries, and so forth, is, as we have seen, a late development. And furthermore, it seems to me, this restriction is in some fundamental sense arbitrary with regard to its extension. That is, it corresponds to no conspicuous or important property of the things it picks out. This, I believe, is fundamentally because such concepts as "disinterested pleasure," "significant form," and so forth—the key terms of the differentiated art world—actually do not refer. There is simply *no such thing* as disinterested pleasure or significant form. More controversially, there may also be no such thing as genius, or primordial emotional expression. What the differentiated art world represents, rather than a certain line of conceptual or experiential development, is the history of certain class relations, the elaborate development of snobbery into a systematic ideology which finally gets fossilized into institutions. What the differentiated art world is about is exclusion, exclusion based not on conceptual, but finally on social and institutional grounds. Its attempts to destroy itself arise out of self-loathing for that exclusion.

The conceptual emptiness of differentiated art is evident in the definitions of "work of art" which most closely approach extensional adequacy with regard to works of art in the aesthetic sense: the institutional view associated with Dickie, Levinson's or Carroll's historical approaches, and the structure of consciousness view that I am attributing here to Danto. The latest permutation of Dickie's view is that "a work of art is an artifact of a kind created to be presented to an artworld public."[12] Levinson writes that "an artwork is a thing (item etc.) that has been seriously intended for regard-as-a-work-of-art, i.e. regard (treatment etc.) in any way preexisting artworks have are or were correctly regarded, so that an experience of some value be thereby obtained."[13] Both these definitions (like Danto's) seem to be circular, though both Dickie and Levinson have fended off that criticism (or in Dickie's case, embraced it) heroically. But the real problem of circularity is not conceptual but, let us say, political. Each of these definitions turns high art back on itself for its own validation as art; each asserts that only what falls into a certain history or a certain institutional framework (the institutional framework and history of the Western fine arts) is art. That, however, is not how the *Western* term 'work of art' *is* used, as we have seen.

More importantly, however, each of these theories is an elaborate suggestion, it seems to me, that there *is* nothing that all and only works of art in the aesthetic sense have in common but the fact that they are housed in certain buildings, that they take their place in a certain historical development, or that they are in some sense about themselves and each other. Each of them starts with the miserable failure of various aesthetic definitions: expressionist theories, formalist views, and so forth. And each of them is a description of the emptiness and narcissism at the heart of avant-garde art, an emptiness which has led the avant-garde into its paroxysms of self-destruction.

Each of them, finally, takes the heart of art to lie in a certain sort of self-awareness, whereas art occurs just as frequently, and more deeply and authentically, in situations in which self-awareness is lost in absorption.

IV

Abstract painting tried to achieve an ontological breakthrough by making paintings into real things. The funny thing about this is that paintings already *were* real things: canvases covered with pigments. In other words, all the prodigious effort expended to make paintings into real things was in a sense very comical: a herculean attempt to achieve what was already obviously the case. All that was really required was an acknowledgment of the way things already were. I think we need to work out ways of reintegrating the arts into people's lives. But the mode of reintegration I want to put forward is simply that we acknowledge what is already the case: the arts are *already* fully integrated into people's lives. The remainder of this book is an attempt to show that this is the case and to help us in recovering our sense of the artistry of the things around us.

Every attempt of the avant-garde to destroy itself only differentiates, identifies, and strengthens it. If the art of this century teaches us anything at all, it is that putting junked cars or comic books into the museum does not destroy the museum, it only makes curators more conscious of themselves as curators, and museum-goers more conscious of themselves as museum-goers. So I suggest that, rather than attack the avant-garde, or radicalize it further (if that is possible), we ignore it to death. The avant-garde should appreciate this, since they have been trying to get rid of one another for decades. To reintegrate art fully into the life of the culture does not entail breaking down the walls of the museum, or issuing broadsides against useless aesthetic objects including artists, it entails only *noticing* the things around us that are well and truly made. Indeed, one can picture an avant-garde happening that actually consisted of blowing up the Museum of Modern Art. If that were to happen, the Museum of Modern Art would be, more than ever, a shrine of the aesthetic: people would come and disinterestedly ogle the rubble. The artist Chris Burden has come close to doing exactly that.

We could come to regard the well-made things around us as art. This would be to cure our aesthetic estrangement by showing that the aesthetic estrangement of the culture as a whole rests on a mistake, or does not exist. Think, for example, of automobiles. Cars are something many people of the west experience every day. And many models (I exclude my 1982 Chrysler) are paradigms of skilled making. Literally thousands of parts are fitted together in such a way as to yield a beautiful object, one that is especially well-suited to make the experience, say, of commuting to work, or of taking the kids to visit their grandparents, inherently satisfying. An acknowledgment of the artfulness of cars would call into question a host of the assumptions of the differentiated artworld: that art is individual (cars are collaborations of designers, engineers, production-line workers, and so forth), that it is found only in certain institutions, that the making of art is non- or antitechnological. All of these are assumptions that the avant-garde has itself been trying to attack, but each such attack is subject to co-optation.

Finally, let me simply suggest a range of items and processes we might come to regard as art, or more insistently emphasize as art, since some of them are regarded as art already: clothing, child-rearing, tattooing, sport, cookery, pedagogy. As is so often the case, making progress here does not mean obtaining what we do not have but coming to appreciate what we have already. The full integration of the arts into the life of this culture is not a dream; it is already a fact.

Notes

1. Arthur Danto, "The End of Art," *The Philosophical Disenfranchisement of Art* (New York: Columbia University Press, 1986), 107.

2. John Wilcox, "The Beginnings of L'art Pour L'art," *The Journal of Aesthetics and Art Criticism* 11 (June 1953): 360–377.

3. Quoted in ibid., 360.

4. Théophile Gautier, *Mademoiselle de Maupin* (Paris, 1834), 22. Translated in Iredell Jenkins, "Art for Art's Sake," *The Dictionary of the History of Ideas* (New York: Charles Scribner's Sons, 1968), 110.

5. Gustave Flaubert and George Sand, *Flaubert-Sand: The Correspondence*, trans. Frances Steegmuller and Barbara Bray (New York: Knopf, 1993).

6. Walter Pater, *The Renaissance* (Oxford: 1873), 239.

7. Clive Bell, *Art* (London: Chatto and Windus, 1914), p.27.

8. Clement Greenberg, "Avant-garde and Kitsch," *Art and Culture* (Boston: Beacon Press, 1961), 5, 6.

9. Ellsworth Kelly, in "Matisse: A Symposium," *Art in America* 81, no. 5 (May 1993): 76.

10. One or another of the Futurist manifestoes, quoted in Joshua Taylor, *Futurism* (New York: Doubleday, 1961), 11.

11. See John Dewey, *Art as Experience* (New York: Minton, Balch, and Co., 1934), chapter 1. Hans-Georg Gadamer, *Truth and Method* (New York: Crossroad, 1985), part 1.

12. George Dickie, "The New Institutional Theory of Art," in *Aesthetics: A Critical Anthology*, ed. George Dickie, Richard Sclafani, and Ronald Roblin (New York: St. Martin's Press, 2nd edition 1989), 204.

13. Jerrold Levinson, "Refining Art Historically," *The Journal of Aesthetics and Art Criticism* 47 (Winter 1989): 29.

Chapter 5

Art and Tradition in American Popular Music

Most people in America and Europe listen to music every day; they watch music videos, listen to background music in stores or on television, or hear country or rock or classical music on their car radios. That's one reason why exotic strategies for reintegrating art into the everyday life of Western culture are unnecessary. If you want to drive the avant-garde insane (this, on the account of the avant-garde itself, is redundant), stop spending your money in galleries and start going out two-stepping to the music of Hank Williams, Jr. Hank makes traditional American art, and he makes it well. He practices a *technē*, in other words. And he sings about life in the culture, not the Ride of the Valkyries. His music is about drinking, divorce, celebrating, driving, fighting. It is not about the nature of art. And his music is already all around us. Again, our culture is permeated with music, whether it is Hank, or the Mississippi Mass Choir, or Ice Cube, or Metallica. Much of this is, I think, great music, and American popular music has invigorated the music of the world. It is interesting to watch pure musical form unfolding in Schubert, say. But it is directly *involving* to buy Metallica's CDs, tattoo yourself like the band, and thrash. That, I propose, is a deeper and more profound experience of art than is listening to Cage's silence.

Now I suppose that it will be said that the integration of such music into our lives does *not* constitute the integration of art into those lives, because that music is not art, or is aesthetically debased art, or is merely popular art. This chapter is devoted to attacking such claims. There are two other, related claims that I want to use this material to question. First, as we have seen, the aesthetics of art for art's sake, the aesthetics of the avant-garde, is fundamentally hostile to tradition. Greenberg, for one, argued that the avant-garde is necessary precisely as an escape from tradition. Now most art that has been made in the world celebrates and enacts tradition. And, in fact, most art in *our* culture does so. I think that a discussion of such enduring popular arts as the blues and country music will show this to be the case. This brings us to the second point in question, namely the claim that Western culture is rootless, that, by and large, it lacks enduring traditions. I want to use blues and country music to demonstrate that such claims are false, or at least in need of careful qualification.

Richard Shusterman, in his exemplary discussion of funk and hip hop in relation to pragmatist aesthetics, says this:

> The strongest and most urgent reason for defending popular art is that it provides us (even us intellectuals) with too much aesthetic satisfaction to accept its wholesale denunciation as debased. To condemn it as fit only for the barbaric taste and dull wit of the unenlightened, manipulated masses is to divide us not only against the rest of our community but against ourselves. We are made to disdain the things that give us pleasure and to feel ashamed of the pleasure they give.[1]

I view popular arts, and in particular popular musics, as the most vital and the most culturally resonant arts of contemporary America. And I regard the wholesale attacks on such arts (where they are not, as is usual with country music, regarded as beneath contempt) by intellectuals as diverse as Adorno and Allan Bloom, as insufferable snobbery. Furthermore, I regard the technological media, by which these musics are to some extent disseminated, with great affection. But my fundamental reason to include this lengthy discussion of blues and country is the same as Shusterman's; I seek to acknowledge the quality and depth of my own appreciations. If I were to restrict myself to, say, discussions of Shostakovich, and then go home and listen to Aaron Tippin singing "Working Man's Ph.D.," I would be a hypocrite. This chapter, then, is a defense of my own preferences. But it is also a defense of the basic modes of artistic production and dissemination in our culture, modes which are ubiquitous, questionable, and also tremendous fun.

Dewey and the Blues
(written with Douglas R. Anderson)

Dewey's aesthetics, which I have mentioned before as a primary inspiration of the theory of art presented in the first part of this book, can be used as a way of explicating and defending the aesthetic importance of the African-American musical form known as the blues. Musicologists, ethnologists, and students of popular culture have long recognized the importance of this music. Nevertheless, philosophers of art have displayed a marked resistance to considering blues—or any other folk or popular musical form—as providing central cases of art. Thus, there is not much discussion of such forms in the literature of aesthetics.[2] We hope to formulate a defense of the artfulness of the blues, and by implication, of popular musical forms—such as country, hip hop, soul, and rock—that are, to a large extent, based on the blues.

By extension, and in the service of the program of aesthetic integration described in the last chapter, we will argue that there is no defensible distinction between fine and "folk" art, and that the aesthetic products of marginalized cultures may have a particular claim to artistic legitimacy in a situation in which "fine art" operates in part as a form of cultural imperialism. In particular, the conception of art as the property of an avant-garde leads to the devaluation of traditional arts, wherein continuity with the past is valued at least as highly as originality of expression. The blues is a fundamental structure, one that undergirds much of the popular music of this century in much of the world. So to a certain extent, our argument can be generalized. But the blues is also the achievement of a particular people, and has particular resonance within the culture that produced it. It is in that context, and indeed in part for that reason, that the blues is an important art.

I

At the beginning of *Art as Experience*, Dewey describes and decries the progressive alienation of art from everyday human activities which marks the Western tradition, and which was described at length in the last chapter. Dewey writes:

> When an art product once attains classic status, it somehow becomes isolated from the human conditions under which it was brought into being and from the human consequences it engenders in actual life-experience. When artistic objects are separated from both conditions of origin and operation in experience, a wall is built around them that renders almost opaque their general significance, with which esthetic theory deals.[3]

Dewey, as we have seen, terms this the "compartmentalization" of art, and he relates it to wider philosophical and social changes. He asserts that it is the fundamental task of philosophers of art to seek a rapprochement between the aesthetic and everyday experience.

The compartmentalization of art reflects, Dewey argues, the fear of the senses and the devaluation of the body in our epistemology and metaphysics, a fear and devaluation that I will discuss more elaborately in the next chapter. "For many persons," he writes, "an aura of mingled awe and unreality encompasses the 'spiritual' and the 'ideal' while 'matter' has become in contrast a term of depreciation, something to be explained away and apologized for" (*Art as Experience*, p. 6). Thus, on the view Dewey attacks, the work of art, if it is to be regarded as valuable, must not be treated as a mere presentation to sense. On the contrary, art should be regarded as the sensuous channel to the spiritual. Hegel, for example, writes that "the sensuous is *spiritualized* in art."[4] So art needs to be given a special status; it is supposed to be the occasion not of desire and sensuous enjoyment but of "disinterested pleasure" (Kant), "pure, will-less knowing" (Schopenhauer), or "psychical distance" (Bullough). The proper response to Titian's *Venus of Urbino*, for example, is not sexual arousal, despite the fact that it is perhaps the most obvious fact about such a work that it is intended to evoke precisely that response.

As we have seen, the compartmentalization of art that Dewey describes is no metaphor. Art is literally gathered up and deposited in museums, in a physical simulacrum of aesthetic distance. This is, Dewey asserts, to a large extent a reflection of class relations; the upper classes treat art as a badge of superior status, and erect museums as an expression of the spirituality of the culture's upper crust. "An instructive history of modern art could be written in terms of the formation of the distinctively modern institutions of museum and exhibition gallery" (*Art as Experience*, p. 8). And he continues: "It erects these buildings and collects their contents as it now builds a cathedral. These things reflect and establish superior cultural status, while their segregation from the common life reflects the fact that they are not part of the native and spontaneous culture" (p. 9).

This critique of the gap between "fine art" and "spontaneous culture" and of the practices of exhibition and criticism which attend it, was prescient. Philosophers such as Nelson Goodman and Hans-Georg Gadamer have made precisely the same attacks on the notion of distance and on the museum system. Goodman, for example, writes:

> [T]he circumstances for viewing in a museum are at best abnormal and adverse. The viewer cannot handle a work, try it in different lights, put it beside various other works for comparison, take it home, come upon it in a sunbeam reflected from snow, contemplate it in comfort. The floors in a museum will defeat any feet and wrack any back; the distance from turnstile to object you want to see is longer than from airport

entrance to your flight; the displays are as if congealed in a glass paperweight, the lighting as unvarying as in summer at the Poles, the oases as scarce as in Death Valley, and the atmosphere as bristling with prohibitions as the Pentagon.[5]

This is the institutional embodiment of the concept of art for art's sake that we traced in the last chapter: art that has been yanked from its context and which is thus no longer capable of transforming that context. The art experience in a museum is at once intensified by being isolated and deflected by being separated from everyday life.[6]

II

As was pointed out in the last chapter, there are two routes by which we might hope to attack the segregation and alienation of art that is represented by the museum. One is to produce works of art aimed at the gallery and museum system which themselves undermine the presuppositions of that system. That strategy has already proven itself to be a failure. We now want to give a full-scale example of the other strategy: experiencing and celebrating the art that is already all around us. The contrast of the museum to, say, a blues club in Chicago or Memphis could not be more striking. People in the club are laughing, yelling, dancing. They are in direct interchange with the artists and with each other. They have joined together in a shared festival. And they are enjoying good, sometimes great, art.

That Dewey recognizes this mode of integration is suggested by the following passage: "The arts which today have the most vitality for the average person are things he does not take to be arts: for instance, the movie, jazzed music, the comic strip. . . . For, when what he knows as art is relegated to the museum and gallery, the unconquerable impulse towards experiences enjoyable in themselves finds such outlet as the daily environment provides" (*Art as Experience*, pp. 5, 6). Now Dewey bemoans this situation because he thinks such occasions for aesthetic experience are "cheap and vulgar," though they are the only outlets for the aesthetic impulse when great art has been consigned to the connoisseur. However, it is appropriate to point out that there is an internal tension in this account. Insofar as such things as jazz and comic strips are indeed the occasions for esthetic experience—that is, for Dewey, experience that displays coherence, that has rhythm and consummation rather than mere procedure and cessation—and insofar as they reflect the vitality of the culture as a whole, it is hard to see how Dewey himself could dismiss them as vulgar. The word 'vulgar' enshrines the very class distinctions that Dewey is elsewhere concerned to attack. Dewey indeed suggests at several points that it is a consequence of his aesthetics that the distinction between fine and popular art breaks down.

As Dewey argues in *Experience and Nature*: "the history of human experience is a history of the development of arts" (p. 388). And he writes:

> Esthetic, fine art, appreciation, drama have a eulogistic flavor. We hesitate to call the penny-dreadful work of fiction artistic, so we call it debased fiction or a travesty on art. Most sources of direct enjoyment for the masses are not art to the cultivated, but perverted art, an unworthy indulgence. Thus we miss the point. A passion of anger, a dream, a relaxation of the limbs after effort, swapping of jokes, horse-play, beating of drums, blowing of tin whistles, explosion of firecrackers and walking on stilts, have the same quality of immediate and absorbing finality that is possessed by things and acts dignified by the title of esthetic. (*Experience and Nature*, p. 80).

If we take this claim seriously, we need also to take seriously aesthetic products that are excluded from the usual canon of fine art.

One particularly promising procedure in this regard is to acknowledge as art the aesthetic products of subcultures that have been marginalized within the larger society. Such marginalization results in the construction of barriers of access to differentiated art. For example, the African-American population of the South at the end of the nineteenth century and the beginning of the twentieth had very little access to the masterpieces housed in museums. Those masterpieces were not only literally difficult to view, they were difficult to understand because they were products of the alien, European culture. The works of, say, the post-impressionists were both inaccessible and probably uninteresting to Mississippi sharecroppers. Indeed, one might almost say that they were *designed* to be uninteresting to such people. They were saturated with theory, products of a sophisticated context. In a word, they were projected into the atmosphere of aesthetic differentiation; they only revealed their meaning to the initiated, and understanding them was itself a token of initiation. The experience embodied in such works may well be intense and satisfying, but it is also in some ways shallow, and it reflects elitist origins; its intended audience is limited to initiates, and it addresses (or at any rate, is held to address) only a fragment of the person who views it. That is, it is held that such works address the "aesthetic faculty."

By contrast, works which arise spontaneously within a culture are almost universally comprehensible within that culture as a whole; they reflect the vitality of the whole culture, and embody its experience. And they engage the members of that culture physically and emotionally; they have specific relevance to the "ideas and affairs" of everyday life.

The systematic racial segregation that followed Reconstruction in the last two decades of the nineteenth century was deplorable for many reasons; political and economic disenfranchisement were fossilized into institutions and legitimized by law. But by the same token, this situation allowed, or constrained, African-American culture to develop in relative isolation from white America, and vice versa. Various art forms developed as expressions of African-American culture, and in particular astonishingly vital musical forms were generated: blues, jazz, gospel, and ragtime among them. The importance of these is reflected in the claim of LeRoi Jones (later Amiri Baraka) that "if the Negro represents, or is symbolic of, something in and about the nature of American culture, this certainly should be revealed by his characteristic music."[7] Indeed, one way to understand a culture is by examining what it systematically excludes. African-American musical forms drew both on European and African antecedents, but arose also in response to specific conditions, and gathered independent momentum. (The basic way the music was and is *used* in celebratory contexts, is fundamentally African.) In fact, their momentum was so great that they propelled American (and even British and European) popular music as a whole for more or less the entire century after they emerged from the subculture that produced them.

II

The art that has most resonance in people's experience arises organically from the culture in response to the conditions in which the culture operates. The blues, it is believed, emerged first of all from the group work songs of slavery, and from the isolated field hollers of sharecroppers who, in the late nineteenth century, worked separate patches of land on behalf of plantation owners. As Gilbert Chase puts it, drawing from the work of John and Alan Lomax, "When a lonely Negro man plowing out in some hot, silent river bottom, raised his voice in a wailing 'cornfield holler,' he was singing the birth of the blues."[8] The style developed into a codified, indeed quite narrow form, in the second decade of this century, and a group of professional performers was generated who played at barrel houses and parties throughout the rural South. This laid the groundwork for the "classic" blues of Ma Rainey, Bessie Smith, and others. As the African-American population moved northward and into urban areas, the blues did likewise, adapting itself to new themes and new instruments relevant to the context. The themes reflected the changing economic and social role of the African-American as the nation as a whole reorganized itself. As Jones says, the "limited social and emotional alternatives of the work song could no longer contain the growing experience of this country that Negroes began to respond to" (*Blues People*, p. 62). It is worth emphasizing that the notion that a blues song "contains," rather than, say, reflects, an experience would be profoundly congenial to Dewey. And again, this music has affected the popular styles of much of the world. W.E.B. Du Bois wrote in 1903:

> And so by fateful chance the Negro folk-song—the rhythmic cry of the slave—stands today not simply as the sole American music, but as the most beautiful expression of human experience, born this side of the seas. It has been neglected, it has been, and is, half despised, and above all it has been persistently mistaken and misunderstood; but notwithstanding, it still remains as the singular spiritual heritage of the nation and the greatest gift of the Negro people.[9]

Avant-garde or "differentiated" art in the romantic/modernist sense, as we have seen, pits itself against the culture as a whole and views itself as the product of an elite group of highly original "geniuses." This generates the myth of the isolated artist struggling to embody a Promethean originality. And though Dewey believes that the products of such artists may be paradigms of the esthetic, they gain this status in spite of the artistic pose of their creators, or at any rate in opposition to the mythology of creation that the modernist artworld imposes on them retrospectively. For Dewey (as well as for Gadamer), art must not be isolated from the culture that produces it; indeed, art is a way of uniting a culture by communication among its members rather than splintering a culture into avant-garde and kitsch: "the expressions that constitute art are communication in its pure and undefiled form. Art breaks through barriers that divide human beings which are impermeable in ordinary association" (*Art as Experience*, p. 224).

Whereas "modern" art defines itself by rejection of the tradition and the culture in which it is all the time embedded (and thus proceeds by a series of "revolutions"), the blues is a perfect example of a traditional art form. Though certain blues artists are lionized, and though some are highly original, they are lionized as the exemplars of the tradition and they are original in the sense that they extend (rather than reject) the tradition. That is, the individuality of their work never self-consciously attempts to distort or destroy the continuity of their culture, but reflects some mode of its organic development, so that the "intensely personal nature of blues-singing is also the result of what can be called the Negro's 'American experience'" (Jones, *Blues People*, p. 66). Indeed, the blues is an enduring tradition; such artists as Son Seals, Billy Branch, Saffire, William Clarke, and Robert Cray can express their distinctive experience by the use of song forms and even specific licks devised in the 1930's or earlier. The extension of tradition can be heard, for example, in jazz's use of instruments to capture, rather than override, the vocal element of the blues. Consider, for example, the expressive effects achieved by the *voice* of Louis Armstrong's trumpet. This is true also in the blues proper, where one of the main traditional instruments is the harmonica, which is cheap, portable, and very close in timbre to the human voice. Indeed, many blues harp players can make their instrument "talk"; Sonny Terry makes his say "mama." Similar effects are achieved on the guitar, for instance by B.B. King on Lucille, his personified instrument. In maintaining the direct connection to the human voice even in instrumentals, jazz and the blues refuse the move from the physical to the spiritual that Dewey sees as the motivation for much modern art practice. And compare the roughness and individuality of blues and jazz singers such as Billie Holiday, Howling Wolf, and Magic Sam to the "trained" voices of the classical tradition. This roughness is essential to an immediately comprehensible emotional expression. The blues was often rejected as "sinful," and was felt to be overtly sexual even in cases where sexuality was not a theme. This reaction illustrates both the fear of the senses that Dewey locates at the heart of modern art, and the celebration of the senses in the blues.

This sense of physical celebration is very much present also, perhaps surprisingly, in African-American sacred music. If you have ever seen a mass choir in action, you know what we mean: people are dancing, raising their hands in supplication or thanksgiving, and singing with total embodiment. Performers such as Aretha Franklin and James Brown, performers who are as compelling as any singers in any musical genre of this century, owe their basic feel to gospel. Even in the secular context, their performances still involve a direct sense of inspiration that is ultimately African in origin, and is shared by African-American clergymen and choir leaders all over the country: their performances are unpredictable, volatile, and riveting. The audience in an African-American gospel church is not well distinguished from the performers: all are fully participating in worship together. This too recalls African ritual. Contrast this, again, with the polite silence of a European or European-American church, or, for that matter, with a concert hall where "classical" music is being performed. In the African-American tradition of sacred music, music allows the spirit to be experienced as immanent in the body, where it now finds external expression. As John Lee Hooker says: "Let the boy boogie-woogie. It's in him and it's got to come out."

It is possible to trace not only themes but phrases and verses from early blues to the present. Such phrases as "easy rider" (C.C. Rider, see see rider), "dust my broom," and "meat shakin' on my bones" have survived in various contexts (and sometimes with distinct or variant meanings) within the blues tradition. And themes such as labor, lust, violence, poverty, and substance abuse have endured from the inception of the blues to the birth of its most recent popular descendant, hip hop. Such themes by their nature cannot be treated in abstract or non-physical terms. The explicitness of these themes and the ways in which they are addressed are remarkably continuous in the African-American musical tradition from the blues to rap. Here are some lines from Muddy Waters's "Mannish Boy":

When I was a young boy at the age of five,
My mother said I was gonna be the greatest man alive.

Now I'm a man, way past twenty-one,
I want you to believe me, baby, I have lots of fun.
I'm a man. I spell "M," "A" child, "N" . . .
I'm a natural-born lover man . . .
I'm a hoochie-coochie man.

Compare that to this from the contemporary rap artist Kool Moe Dee:

Ice water, watch your daughter,
Your mother and your sisters, nieces and wife oughtta
    know,
Ain't nobody safe when I'm in the place . . .
Just wait for double black to double back
And make that move, break it to ya, I'm a do ya . . .
You can feel the heat but there ain't no pressure.
When I turn the heat on the cool breeze will refresh ya.
How cool, how cool, how cool can one black man be?

In contrast, "Modern" art defines itself as the exploration of the terms of the medium for its own sake. Painting, for example, comes to be about painting in the works of Pollock and others. But the blues is a response to and elucidation of the conditions of the culture as a whole. The blues is about poverty, floods, murder, love, strutting, drinking, and sinking, not as distant or ideal themes, but as elements of the lived experience of African-Americans. When Lonnie Brooks sings "inflation done give me the blues," or when Robert Johnson sings "there's a hellhound on my trail," they speak of the world they encounter. It is precisely this "truthful" organicism of the blues that is sometimes absent when white musicians attempt to appropriate the style but not the experience which it reflects; thus, Eric Clapton or Benny Goodman are blues or jazz musicians precisely to the extent that these forms can be appropriated to represent *their own* cultural experience.[10] Julio Finn, in *The Bluesman*, points out what can hardly be denied, that many whites (he mentions Paul Butterfield, the J. Geils Band, the Allman Brothers, Charlie Musselwhite, and Johnny Winter, among others) play the blues expertly. "However," he writes, "they can never be *bluespeople*. Why not? Because the blues is not something they *live* but something they *do*—which makes all the difference in the world."[11] They cannot, in other words, be African-American bluespeople, though they may constitute a group of white bluespeople, who appropriate the form of the blues to their own cultural and personal circumstances. And against Finn, we might point out that though white and black cultures in America are distinct, they overlap in many ways as well, and that the appropriation of the blues to represent the cultural experience of whites is, hence, not a total removal from context.

Art in Dewey's sense presupposes an organic connection to a culture, and an organic expression of that culture; art is not merely something people do, but something they live. Jones traces this organicism to African antecedents: "It was, and is, inconceivable in African culture to make a separation between music, dancing, song, the artifact, and man's life or his worship of gods. *Expression* issued from life, and *was* beauty" (*Blues People*, p. 29) The blues reflects these elements of its African antecedents. It is a living art, and an art of living.

III

W. C. Handy, who was the first person to publish a blues song, wrote:

> In its origin, modern blues is the expression of the emotional life of a race. In the south of long ago, whenever a new man appeared to work in any of the laborers' gangs, he would be asked if he could sing. If he could, he got the job. The singing of these working men set the rhythm of the work, the pounding of hammers, the winging of scythes; and the one who sang most lustily soon became strawboss. One man set the tune, and sang whatever sentiments lay closest to his heart. He would sing about steamboats, fast trains, "contrairy" mules, cruel overseers. If he had no home, he sang about that; if he found a home the next day, he sang about needing

money or being lonesome for his gal. But whatever he sang was personal, and then the others in the gang took up the melody, each fitting it with personal words of his own. If fifty men worked on the gang, the song had fifty verses, and the singing lasted all day through, easing the work, driving rhythm into it.[12]

For Dewey, the transformation of an activity that is performed mechanically to one that displays rhythm and coherence is a transformation to the aesthetic. The blues never remained in a sealed aesthetic chamber awaiting delectation; rather, it constantly arose out of and transformed people's day to day existence into something meaningful, "drove rhythm into it." It both told and wove its way into the story of a people; it embodied and transformed a culture. Work became art.

Art is, to repeat, a matter not of what is done, but of how what is done is done. It is possible, though barely, to imagine the most back-breaking physical toil as an art. If we try to imagine this, we might try to imagine the adornment of this activity with music. But note: if we are to imagine gang labor adorned with music, we must think of the adornment in Coomaraswamy's terms, as the completion of function, as a potentializing and actualizing agent within the activity and its object. For the adornment of music does not merely make dehumanizing labor appear more attractive or charming; it transforms both the activity and its product at the deepest level. Repetitive manual labor without song is too often drudgery. But manual labor with song is something that calls for our immersion. And manual labor with collective song is involving, loving, perhaps even playful. The same is true of the function of music, say, in driving: the conversion of a mechanical activity to something one can participate in and enjoy.

While it is important to examine how specific elements of music reflect or embody specific styles of life, it is equally important to see how blues (as well as jazz, rhythm and blues, soul, rap, and so forth) has described the institutional continuity of the African-American's status in America. "It seems possible," Jones says, "that some kind of graph could be set up using samplings of Negro music proper to whatever moment of the Negro's social history was selected, and that in each grouping of songs a certain frequency of reference could pretty well determine his social, economic, and psychological states at that particular period" (*Blues People,* p. 65). The blues is an expression of oppression (and for just that reason has been rejected by some blacks, who regard it as a badge of subservience): "blues could not exist if the African captives had not become American captives" (*Blues People* p. 17). At the same time, the blues is a *response* to oppression. Blues, that is to say, is not merely "sad" in some superficial sense. Rather, it is at once the expression of and the treatment for a deep sadness accomplished by a culture. It is a rising out of oppression, but it is a rising in which the oppression is preserved as a fact, in which the sadness of the reality is allowed to be at the same time that is transcended. It is at once mournful and celebratory. It provides occasions to dance and drink the blues away, and often contains a barely hidden protest about prevailing conditions of poverty and exclusion. So while it arises in a cultural context, blues also seeks to ameliorate—and occasionally transform—that context; it is both organic and subversive. There is no more telling illustration of this than Frederick Douglass's account of the hollers that lie at the root of the blues:

> I did not, when a slave, understand the deep meaning of those rude and apparently incoherent songs. I was myself within the circle; so that I neither saw nor heard as those without might see and hear. They told a tale of woe which was then altogether without my feeble comprehension; they were tones loud, long, and deep; they breathed the prayer and complaint of souls boiling over with the bitterest anguish. Every tone was a testimony against slavery, and a prayer to God for a deliverance from chains. The hearing of those wild notes always depressed my spirits and filled me with ineffable sadness.[13]

The blues embodies into rhythm and melody the experience of a people. Art has no higher calling.

Confucius and Country Music

I turn now to country music, in recognition and celebration of the traditions of American culture. My basic orientation to tradition is drawn from Confucius, who of all the great thinkers of world history is the most aware of the pervasiveness and power of cultural tradition. I take as my text book XI, chapter 1 of the *Analects*, which reads, in D. C. Lau's translation:

> The Master said, "As far as the rites and music are concerned, the disciples who were the first to come to me were rustics while those who came to me afterwards were gentlemen. When it comes to putting the rites and music to use, I follow the former."[14]

I take this to mean that Confucius respected the musical tastes of the rustics, or, as we would put it, that Confucius enjoyed country music.

Indeed, Confucius was both a musician and a connoisseur of music; music is central to the *Analects*.[15] In the following passage, for example, Confucius uses music as a metaphor for a social arrangement kept in place by the observance of traditional *li* (rites):

> This much can be known about music. It begins with playing in unison. When it gets into full swing, it is harmonious, clear, and unbroken. In this way it reaches its conclusion. (III:23, Lau, p. 71)

When a musical ensemble is playing well, it achieves unity and harmony effortlessly. No one has to be constrained or exhorted to play well or to combine his efforts with that of the group. Again, this is an image of a state of social harmony created by the observance of traditional rites. In such a state, no one has to be forced to act harmoniously with the whole; in virtue of one's participation in *li*, one is already in harmony. It has been well said that Confucius's political philosophy is essentially aesthetic, emphasizing a beautiful arrangement of traditional elements.[16] His image of society as musical ensemble lends force to this interpretation. So there is certainly ample justification for discussing Confucius in relation to music in general. I hope to show in what follows that there is justification also for discussing Confucius in relation to American country music in particular.

American culture is more traditional than we might think, and hence a Confucian approach to that culture is not as alien as it might at first glance appear to be. When we focus on the folk and popular arts of American culture, we begin to see that American culture displays considerable continuity, and that the Confucian concept of *li* can help make this clear. Country music is itself an American tradition (as is the blues), but furthermore, country music constantly emphasizes and celebrates tradition in its lyric content. Roughly, I take 'tradition' to refer to relatively enduring cultural practices embodied in a pattern of ritual activity. Country music is, in that sense, a tradition. But what makes country a particularly appropriate example is, as I will show, that it explicitly thematizes the *li* of which it is also an example; that is, it can help us to see, in a variety of ways, how tradition permeates American culture.

I

In their book *Thinking through Confucius*, David Hall and Roger Ames deploy a distinction between "historical" and "traditional" cultures.[17] I will argue that this distinction must be carefully qualified with regard to Western culture when we take the folk and popular arts of that culture seriously as data that have to be accounted for. At any rate, according to Hall and Ames, Western culture is historical, while Chinese culture is traditional. In an historical culture, according to Hall and Ames, there is a special value placed on individuality and its expression. Culture itself is experienced as in some sense and to some degree hostile to the individual's unique experience and the unique embodiment of that experience in intellectual and artistic products. Thus, for example, to be a great philosopher in Western culture is often to be a revolutionary thinker, and philosophy seems to proceed largely by a series of overturnings. This is perfectly exemplified in Descartes, who vowed to forget all previous philosophy, indeed to doubt all the assumptions bequeathed to him by his culture, and to start the project of thinking over again from scratch. (For the moment I leave it an open question to what extent this is possible.) Here we have in capsule the features that Hall and Ames ascribe to an historical culture: the tremendous emphasis on individuality (Descartes works into, and finally out of, solipsism, a procedure that would have been incomprehensible to Confucius), suspicion of the past, advancement through revolutionary overturning.

These aspects of historical culture, as we saw in the last chapter, are especially pronounced in the arts. The ideology of modernism is a particularly virulent form of historical culture, and displays all the features mentioned above to an extreme degree. The artistic culture of the avant-garde is perhaps the best illustration of historical culture in world history. The ultimate sanction on the "true artist" within this culture is, in Ezra Pound's famous phrase, to "make it new."

Indeed, much of modern visual art starting with the impressionists has been accounted for as a series of ever-accelerating revolutions, as a series of "movements," each of which rejects the one before and attempts to start again from scratch. Thus, pop art follows and attacks abstract expressionism, minimalism follows and attacks pop (and abstract expressionism), photo-realism follows and attacks minimalism (and abstract expressionism, and pop), conceptualism follows and attacks photo-realism (and abstract expressionism, and pop, and minimalism), and so forth. If Danto is right, this eventually leads to a situation in which further revolutions become impossible, or in which all revolutions have already taken place; it leads, that is, to the end of historical art. It is relevant to what follows that the same is true to some extent of the avant-garde music of this century. It appears to proceed by radical gestures of rejection of the past (atonality, twelve-tone row construction) in an effort to re-make the present, until, perhaps, it ends in Cage's silence.

Many Western intellectuals tend to try to make sense of their own culture in historical terms, to explain modern Western history as a series of overturnings: as, for example, a dialectical process. I think that, as I will argue, such thinkers underrate and undervalue the traditional elements in their own culture. But there is no doubt that much Western reflection on Western culture emphasizes the discontinuities, the radical breaks, the attempts to reject the past.

By contrast, Hall and Ames describe Chinese culture as traditional. Here, the authenticity of an artist or a thinker cannot be conceptualized in terms of sheer originality or an overcoming of the weight of the past. Indeed, authenticity for the individual is established precisely through a connection with the authentic traditions of the culture. Confucius sets out this view in particular with regard to the observance of traditional *li*, and for precisely this reason, Confucius may appear to be rigid, authoritarian, in short, hide-bound. Indeed, in famous passages, it is said that Confucius refused to sit down unless his mat was oriented correctly (X:12), and it is recommended that one not even move unless it is in accordance with the rites (XII:1). (It must be remarked, however, that this apparent rigidity is qualified in several passages, as in III:4, where Confucius says that "In mourning, it is better to err on the side of grief than on the side of formality" [Lau, p. 67].) This sort of extreme respect for tradition *qua* tradition, for tradition just in virtue of the fact that it is traditional, may appear to Westerners to be extremely problematic, because it abnegates the *critical* approach to the past that they may regard as essential to philosophy, or at any rate, to great philosophers.

Chinese philosophy thus follows a rather different line of development than does Western philosophy. The continuity of the Confucian tradition, for example, is unmatched by any particular tradition of the West. This is not to say, of course, that Confucianism is static; change in that tradition is at times rapid and dramatic. But this change is construed by those who instigate it as an organic unfolding of the existing tradition, rather than its wholesale rejection. To be an influential figure in Confucianism is not to pit oneself against the doctrines of Confucius, but to extend them naturally along certain lines suggested by one's present context. Of course, there is a variety of contrasting movements in early Chinese philosophy; Taoism and Mohism, for example, explicitly reject various elements of Confucian philosophy. But it is an interesting aspect of Chinese intellectual history that it is profoundly syncretic; no sooner are the opposing positions enunciated than people are attempting to combine them into a coherent whole. Later Taoists, for example, seem to feel little pressure to *reject* Confucianism as a whole, nor Confucianists to reject Taoism.

The same contrast of tradition to history could be drawn with respect to the arts. The arts of a traditional culture are by no means static; they undergo development as the society itself adapts to changing circumstances, as we have seen already in the case of the blues. But they always start from a presumption of continuity with the past; a work of art is authentic in virtue of its connection with the tradition. Innovation in the arts takes place through extension of the tradition, in order to bring the tradition to bear within a changed social context, or in order to investigate previously unconceptualized consequences of the tradition (or both). The artistic products of a traditional culture always reflect a phase of that culture in its organic unfolding, rather than a wholesale rejection of the culture.[18] And this is perhaps the most obvious purported difference between the arts in historical and traditional cultures: in the ideology of modernism, for instance, the artist, the genius, is pitted against the culture of average people on the street; they are vulgar, he inspired. (This is absolutely explicit, for example, in Greenberg.) The great modern artist is held to be misunderstood by his contemporaries, incomprehensible to them, ahead of his time, and so forth. In a traditional culture, on the contrary, the artist is engaged in a universally (or at any rate, universally within a certain class) comprehensible mode of communication; she is always a participant in *li*, and in the existing cultural practices.

Indeed, one very important arena in which this distinction plays itself out is that of ritual. In Western cultures, ritual is often regarded as "the husk of true faith," as an empty series of gestures and movements that have been externally prescribed. Religions are criticized for the rigidity of their procedures, which is always an implicit aspersion on the sincerity and self-awareness of the people who perform those procedures. In contrast, in traditional cultures, ritual is loaded with the combined cultural and personal identity—the identity of the individual as a participant in the culture—which is the culture's gift to its members. And it is not a coincidence that whereas most of the art of traditional cultures is made as and for rituals—whereas the spiritual life of the culture is embodied above all in its art—in historical cultures the attempt is made to insulate artmaking from "empty" ritual.

II

I have set out Hall and Ames's distinction between historical and traditional cultures at length. Now I would like to criticize it, or at any rate limit its scope. It is evident, first of all, that, were it to be applied simplistically to Western culture, it would be a caricature. *No* culture could possibly develop along the lines of sheer discontinuity, of constant radical revision, of endless revolution. If this were actually the case, if Western culture did actually proceed along these lines, there would be no sense whatever in the term "Western culture." In fact, I take it to be fairly obvious that Descartes could not have done what he describes himself as doing: as doubting all his assumptions, of getting rid of the vestiges of accreted culture in his philosophy. For even where philosophers or artists attempt to understand their own work as an absolute break with the past, the continuity of their work with the past they purport to reject is always visible retrospectively. Descartes's continuity with the scholastics, for example, is now at least as obvious as his self-conscious rejection of them.

Nevertheless, though I believe that, in a simplistic form, the distinction between traditional and historical cultures is not viable, it is obvious that there *is* a profound difference between the development of avant-garde art and philosophy in the west and the unfolding of traditional arts and philosophies in China. Though we cannot understand, for example, modern art as in fact constantly engaged in a wholesale rejection of the past, we *can* see that certain of its practitioners and certain of its theorists have accounted for Western avant-garde art in precisely these terms. And we can see also that, though the discontinuities of Western culture never appear to be as dramatic in retrospect as they do when they are developed, Western avant-garde culture *is* in fact considerably less continuous than is Chinese culture. So the historical/traditional distinction, properly qualified, does shed interesting light on certain phenomena.

I believe, however, that this distinction, like Danto's narrative of a teleological art history, sheds light only on what I have been calling the "avant-garde" segment of Western culture in distinction from traditional cultures. When we turn our attention toward the full range of artistic products of Western culture—in particular, toward what Greenberg terms "kitsch"—we see, I think, that we in fact live in a culture with many deep-seated and enduring traditions.

For Confucius, the medium of cultural continuity is *li*, the conventional ritual practices of a culture. Here is a chapter of the *Analects* which expresses very clearly the role of *li* in achieving cultural continuity:

> Tzu-Chang asked, "Can ten generations hence be known?"
>
> The Master said, "The Yin built on the rites of the Hsia. What was added and what was omitted can be known. The Chou built on the rites of the Yin. What was added and what was omitted can be known. Should there be a successor to the Chou, even a hundred generations hence can be known." (II:23, Lau, p. 66)

Here again we have the delicate balance, observed throughout the *Analects*, between rigid adherence to *li* and flexible adaptation to changing circumstances. The rites shift with shifting dynasties. But they retain such continuity that "a hundred generations hence can be known." At any rate, one way the distinction between historical and traditional cultures might be framed is precisely in terms of *li*; it might be claimed that Western culture is fundamentally a culture without ceremonies, without a body of entrenched conventions handed down through the generations.

No human culture is without ritual; ritual seems to be a condition of the possibility of culture. But it is always the rituals of one's own culture which are most difficult to bring to awareness. For the true rituals in which one is engaged are simply the direct expressions of a form of life. They are produced, as we saw in the case of the tea ceremony, both perfectly and spontaneously.

One of the many salutary effects of Herbert Fingarette's book *Confucius: The Secular as Sacred*, was that it showed through precise use of examples exactly why the claim that Western culture lacks *li* is false. Fingarette's most elaborately developed example of *li* in Western culture is the ceremonial greeting achieved by shaking hands.[19] Such a greeting brings about a harmony among persons of just the sort that Confucius describes as the effect of *li* in ancient China, and which he compares to the unison of a musical ensemble. You and I shake hands without any awareness of effort, and without any consciousness that we are in fact instantiating an amazingly supple ritual pattern, one with a long tradition in our culture. We are effortless participants in the *li* of Western culture, and we become present to one another in virtue of our participation. The everyday activities of Westerners in the workplace, the dining room, in marriages, child-rearing practices, and so forth, are permeated by rituals, rituals of which the participants are not, for the most part, aware, unless they make a special effort to bring them to consciousness. And Fingarette includes the use of language as a whole among the *li* of Western (and, it might be added, of all other) cultures. Language, after all, is an incredibly elaborate and rich conventional system of behavior, one that is bequeathed to us by our culture. If this extension of *li* to language is indeed legitimate, then much Western social interaction, and indeed much of the thinking of Westerners as individuals, is conditioned by an elaborate system of *li*.

III

Another way to see that Western culture is to a great degree traditional in virtue of the participation of members of that culture in ritual practices is, as I have suggested, to turn our attention to the full range of artistic production in that culture. If we reorient our gaze, for example, from the art that is produced in lofts in Soho to the art that is produced in recording studios in Nashville, we begin to see that tradition may be pervasive in American artistic activities. In fact, country music is enjoyed by a much greater proportion of Americans than is avant-garde art (Greenberg, for example, would have it no other way). And country music constantly emphasizes and depends on a real connection to the lives of those who listen to it.

That is one reason why, if you want to become a country music star, you cannot afford to jettison tradition. A country music artist who rejected the heritage of Jimmie Rodgers, Hank Williams, George Jones, and so forth, would not even be a performer of country music, much less a successful one. Country music, that is to say, instantiates perfectly the pattern of development that Hall and Ames attribute to a traditional culture. Country music is not static; it changes over time and serves somewhat different functions in different contexts, but these changes always supervene on an overriding continuity.

At the end of his song "You Never Even Called Me by My Name," David Allan Coe gives the following recitation:

> A friend of mine named Steve Goodman wrote that song, and he told me it was the perfect country/western song. Well I wrote him back a letter and told him it was not the perfect country/western song because he

hadn't said anything at all about Mama, or trains, or trucks, or prison, or getting drunk.

Coe then proceeds to sing the following verse:

I was drunk the day my mom got out of prison,
And I went to pick her up in the rain.
But before I could get to the station in my pickup truck
She got runned over by a damned old train.

Now this is obviously intended as a parody, but the point is a serious one that no country singer can ignore: certain themes are traditional in country music. These include those enumerated by Coe, and also, I would say, infidelity and divorce.

These themes represent an element of absolute continuity in country music from its origins to the present. Jimmie Rodgers sang about them in the late twenties (for example, in his song "In the Jailhouse Now," which is about drinking, prison, and strained relationships between the sexes). He said at that time: "Folks everywhere are getting tired of all this Black Bottom—Charleston—jazz music junk. They tell me the radio stations keep gettin' more and more calls for old-fashioned songs. . . . Well, I'm ready with them."[20] Bill Monroe, who invented bluegrass music in the 1940's, often said that his goal was to play American music the way it sounded in 1860. Bluegrass, too, is a vital contemporary form. So Rodgers and Monroe regarded themselves as drawing on an already established tradition. Obviously, the artistic traditions of American culture, which is only two or three hundred years old, cannot stretch for thousands of years, as do some Chinese traditions, but country music represents an element of continuity over a considerable stretch of American cultural history, one extending back at least a hundred years. And this tradition itself emerged organically out of European and African musical antecedents. For example, the traditional fiddle-playing that continues today in country music is closely related to Irish reels. And much country music employs a blues tonality that derives from African music such as that of the Yoruba.

It must be remarked, too, that the themes of traditional country music emphasize precisely the rituals bound up with living in American culture. That is why I believe that country music is particularly suited to illustrate the traditional elements of that culture: it not only instantiates, but explicitly addresses and celebrates such traditions. For example, "The Ceremony," a song from the late sixties by George Jones and Tammy Wynette, is a full-scale wedding performed in the recording studio. Here the ritual forms are observed precisely. And the wedding ceremony forms part of the content of many country songs, for example the Randy Travis song "Forever Together." Trials, divorces, parties, and so forth, are all disclosed in country songs in ways that make their ritual content immediately apparent, and in ways which make obvious the role of such rituals in traditional American culture. Indeed, it is partly for this reason that so many people find that country music resonates in their own experience; it emerges out of and enhances the ritual and institutional context in which both the artist and the listener are embedded.

Let us think of ritual in the following way. Rituals are artistic ways of constructing and enacting a culture. That is, rituals are procedures that come to be performed for themselves, come to be experienced as possessing a "rightness" that demands observance. We perform an action in the ritually prescribed way because that is the *right way* to perform it. To perform an action in a ritualistic way (at least in the best case) fixes our attention on the process by which the end of the action is realized. This devotion to process then opens up to us the possibility, or rather it is the very possibility, of sociability. Our devotion to process makes possible an opening to persons, so that culture comes to be embodied in culturally constructive artistic activities. In addition, this devotion to process, to performing our actions in the right way, opens for us the possibility of other devotions. As it calls us out of ourselves, it shows us how to worship, and how to celebrate what we worship. Thus, ritual is bound up with devotion to nature and to gods. Here, the absorption in materials that is the artistic process opens to us a widening series of absorptions: into family, culture, world, and divinity. I will return to this structure of opening in the next chapter.

The culturally significant items of American life—for example, cars, homes, pets, credit cards and country music performers themselves—are constantly exploited as lyrical themes in country music. (Many of these might not appear to be examples of *li*. However, if Fingarette is right, we have to give *li* a very wide scope indeed. And Graham, for example, says that *li* "embraces all rites, custom, manners, conventions."[21]) For example, in "Common Man" John Conlee suggests to his date that they ought to leave the fancy restaurant where they are dining:

> I appreciate your hospitality, but I wish that we could go.
> Let me drive us to McDonald's and let's talk awhile
> Concerning something you should really know.
> I'm a common man, drive a common van.
> My dog ain't got a pedigree.
> If I have my say it's gonna stay that way,
> 'Cause highbrow people lose their sanity.
> And a common man is what I'll be.

Like many country songs, "Common Man" presents an explicit rejection of "highbrow" (or "historical") culture (Alan Jackson: "I like my sushi southern fried"), in order to celebrate the traditions and rituals, of the songwriter's culture, for instance, McDonald's, vans, dogs.

Here is another of Conlee's lyrics:

> Living the domestic life,
> Happy children and a pretty wife,
> Our cocker spaniel's always having puppies.
> How could anybody be so lucky?
> See me mowing my domestic yard.
> Lord I owe my soul to MasterCard.
> But it seems to suit me to a "T."
> The domestic life is alright with me.

Here again, we have an explicit appeal to a wide variety of American traditions and manners (which, to repeat, are not, overall, as enduring as those of Chinese culture, but which lend American society considerable continuity). And if a tradition is a relatively enduring cultural practice embodied in *li*, then these things are American traditions, or are on their way to becoming American traditions. It should be noted that the avant-garde has a habit of sneering at such conventions and customs. But, as I will argue in the last chapter, it would be interesting to be able to relax and enjoy our own rituals, our own technology, our own food, and so forth. This is a world we have built for ourselves, and one which may satisfy many of our desires. Here again, allowing ourselves to celebrate what we already have, and what we already are, is both the most difficult and the only possible approach to our apparent problems.

Another constant theme of country music is country music itself. Among the most frequent references in country music are to country performers, particularly Hank Williams, George Jones, Patsy Cline and Maybelle Carter. These figures are particularly important because they are exemplars of the tradition, and by appealing to them, country music singers both attempt to establish explicitly their credentials as representatives of an ongoing practice, and to celebrate the validity of that practice in virtue of the fact that it *is* traditional. For example, in a recent song, the "new traditionalist" singer/songwriter Alan Jackson sings:

> I've been right here
> Since you've been gone,
> Belly-up at the bottom of a bottle
> Listening to George Jones . . .
> In need an expert on
> The pain I'm going through
> So I'll keep George on the old turntable
> 'Til I'm over you.

George Jones himself puts in a ritual appearance to sing the final verse of the song. This constant appeal for legitimacy to the great figures of the tradition is strikingly similar to the Confucian technique of "creation through transmission." Con-

fucian thinkers starting with Mencius and running throughout Chinese history constantly revert to the Master or to later
exemplars of the tradition, in an attempt to establish the
authenticity of the current thinker's claims.

Mencius himself, in a passage which is central to Confucian thought, and which is based on a very direct extension of
certain passages of the *Analects*, says:

> The actuality of human-heartedness (*jen*) is to serve
> one's parents. The actuality of righteousness (*i*) is to
> obey one's elder brother. The actuality of wisdom
> (*chih*) is this: to know these two things and not to
> depart from them. The actuality of propriety (*li*) is this:
> the ordering and adorning of these two things. The
> actuality of music is this: to rejoice in these two
> things.[22]

If I may be so bold as to offer a loose paraphrase of this passage: wisdom is to know one's social role; propriety is to order
the performance of one's social role through the rites; the purpose of music is to rejoice in one's social role. Country music
constantly exemplifies this function of music. The hit song
"Brotherly Love," for example, by Earl Thomas Conley and
Keith Whitley, is a very precise description and celebration of
relations between an elder and younger brother. Other examples include "Mama Tried," a paean to filial respect (or, more
precisely, an expression of regret over a failure to observe it)
by Merle Haggard, and "Grandpa (Tell Me about the Good
Old Days)," a song by the Judds (written by Jamie O'Hara)
that expresses devotion to elders in virtue of their special
access to tradition.

Lyric themes are not the only element in the continuity of
country. Instrumentation, including guitars, steel guitars,
mandolins, fiddles, and banjos, has remained extremely con-
sistent, even as it has adapted to changes in musical technology (particularly various forms of electronic amplification).
Similarly, song structure is essentially unchanged over at least
sixty years (though country music contains a variety of such
structures): Marty Brown's recent "Ole King Kong" is cribbed

directly from Jimmie Rodgers. Such practices might be held to constitute plagiarism in the avant-garde arts, and would, for theorists such as Greenberg, immediately cast suspicion on the artist as inauthentic. They have just the opposite effect in the context of country music, in which such enactive practices serve precisely to *establish* authenticity for the artist.

In addition, country music performances contain many ritualistic elements, some of which are strikingly parallel to Confucius' discussions of *li*. For example, at X:6, Confucius gives an elaborate set of prescriptions for ritual dress. These prescriptions might be considered quaint relics. But the prescriptions for the clothes of a country singer are no less rigid, and no less elaborate. For example, the "new traditionalism" of Brown, Jackson, Clint Black, and others is often termed "hat music," because its practitioners all wear cowboy hats when performing. A cowboy hat has no practical purpose in a nightclub; it is merely a ritual accessory establishing the place of the performer within the tradition. And the same can be said of sequined jackets, boots, blue jeans, and so forth, as well as the Western outfits worn by such female performers as Patty Loveless and the Sweethearts of the Rodeo.

IV

The ancient Confucian philosopher Hsün Tzu attributed almost supernatural powers to music:

> When it is performed within the household, and father and sons, elder and younger brothers listen to it together, there are none who are not filled with a spirit of harmonious kinship. And when it is performed in the community, and old people and young people listen to it, there are none who are not filled with the spirit of harmonious obedience. Hence music brings about complete unity and induces harmony.[23]

Music for Hsün Tzu was the great agent of social coherence in ancient China (and that was his response to Mo Tzu, who argued that music was a useless luxury). This may sound alien to us, but it worth saying that, in America at the present time, music is also one of the most powerful agents of social cohesion. What you listen to, whether it's "classic rock," heavy metal, rap, classical, swing, bop, "alternative," or country, expresses not just a musical preference, but an entire cultural identification and orientation. Styles of dress, for example, flow from musical preferences. Generational identification is accomplished through the music of the relevant era. Racial identification is accomplished through music. Identification by economic class is accomplished by music. We are already held together and pulled apart as a culture by our music as much as by anything.

That shows that we do not, in order to reintegrate the arts into our culture, need to change what we are doing; we simply need to change how we are thinking about what we are doing. The notion of aesthetic distance and its institutional and disciplinary correlates—art history, the museum, the distinction between art and craft, the distinction between fine and popular art—all of these tend to devalue the most vital arts of our culture. In parallel to this, the story we tell about ourselves in intellectual and social histories denigrates or denies our rituals, which embody the artistic aspect of our life together. But through this whole process, the crafts, the popular arts, and rituals go merrily on; in some ways, indeed, their vitality is aided by their exclusion. The problem, then, is not who we are or what we're doing; the problem is the story we are telling ourselves about who we are and what we're doing. And thus what I am presenting here is not an attack on the fine arts, for example, but an attack on the story we tell ourselves about the fine arts. Much fine art is great art, for example, but surely not because of its distance from us; its greatness would be all the more clear if we could bring it into closer proximity.

Notes

1. Shusterman, *Pragmatist Aesthetics*, (Oxford: Blackwell, 1992), 140.

2. This situation is, however, changing, and has drawn explicit criticism, for example in Shusterman's *Pragmatist Aesthetics* and in David Novitz's *The Boundaries of Art* (Philadelphia: Temple University Press, 1992).

3. Dewey, *Art as Experience*, 3.

4. G. W. F. Hegel, *The Philosophy of Fine Art*, trans. F. P. B. Osmaton, reprinted in *Philosophies of Art and Beauty*, ed. Albert Hofstadter and Richard Kuhns (Chicago: University of Chicago Press, 1976), 409.

5. Nelson Goodman, "The End of the Museum?," *Of Mind and Other Matters* (Cambridge, MA: Harvard University Press, 1984), 174–87. See also Hans-Georg Gadamer, *Truth and Method* (New York: Crossroad, 1985), 78ff.

6. For another angle on this, see John J. McDermott, "To Be Human is to Humanize: A Radically Empirical Aesthetic" in *The Culture of Experience* (New York: New York University Press, 1976), 21–62.

7. LeRoi Jones (Amiri Baraka), *Blues People: Negro Music in White America* (New York: William Morrow & Co., 1968 [1963]), ix.

8. Gilbert Chase, *American Music* (New York: McGraw-Hill, 1955), 452.

9. W. E. B. DuBois, "Of the Sorrow Songs," *The Souls of Black Folk* (Chicago: McClurg & Co., 1904), 251.

10. For an extended treatment of whites and the blues, see Paul Garon, *Blues and the Poetic Spirit* (London: Eddison Press, 1975), 40–61. Garon argues that "'white blues' finds it . . . difficult to exceed the bounds of stupefying mediocrity" (57).

11. Julio Finn, *The Bluesman* (London: Quartet Books, 1986), 229.

12. Quoted in *Readings in Black Southern Music*, ed. Eileen Southern (New York: W.W. Norton, 1983 [1971]), 213.

13. Frederick Douglass, *Narrative of the Life of Frederick Douglass, an American Slave*, (Garden City: Doubleday & Co, Inc., 1963 [1865]), 14.

14. Confucius, *The Analects*, trans. D.C. Lau (New York: Penguin, 1979), 106. It should be remarked that this translation is controversial. However, I use it here as an occasion, rather than as an exegetical fulcrum.

15. See, e.g. VII:14; VIII:8, 15; XIV:12.

16. See, e.g., A. C. Graham, *Disputers of the Tao* (La Salle: Open Court, 1989), 30.

17. David L. Hall and Roger T. Ames, *Thinking through Confucius* (Albany: State University of New York Press, 1987), 21–25.

18. Consider the writings of later Chinese artists and artistic theorists, which almost invariably appeal to the authority of the tradition, for example to Hsieh Ho's six canons of painting. See Lin Yutang, *The Chinese Theory of Art* (London: Heinemann, 1967).

19. Herbert Fingarette, *Confucius: The Secular as Sacred* (New York: Harper and Row, 1972), 9ff.

20. Quoted in *The Illustrated History of Country Music*, ed. Patrick Carr (Garden City: Doubleday, 1979), 53.

21. *Disputers of the Tao*, 11.

22. IVa:27. Trans. Derk Bodde in Fung Yu-lan, *A History of Chinese Philosophy*, vol. 1 (Princeton: Princeton University Press, 1983), 125.

23. *Hsün Tzu: Basic Writings*, trans. Burton Watson (New York: Columbia University Press, 1963), 113.

Chapter 6

The Art of Knowing

One effect of the notion of art for art's sake and of the ideology of modernism is an insulation of the aesthetic from the cognitive. Art, it is claimed, is a presentation to sense, or an expression of emotion, but it is not, or it ought not to be, a source of knowledge. Bell, for example, condemned paintings such as Frith's extravaganzas of Victorian incident on the ground that, while they had much to teach us about the manners of the time, they were not sufficiently interesting as pure form to be considered art. They yielded knowledge, but not aesthetic satisfaction. One practical and immediate result of this insulation has been the devaluing of the arts as educational technique and content. I am going to argue that art is a model of and a method for knowing. Likewise, I will contend that knowing can profitably be considered an art. And I will try to draw out some of the practical implications of these claims.

I

There is a constellation of notions—a constellation associated with epistemological and artistic modernism—which is being challenged both from within philosophy and from within art. In epistemology, these notions include: that knowledge is essentially propositional (that is, that to know is to know some claim to be true); that knowledge requires justification and that justification consists in a logical demonstration from self-evident premises (this requirement has been loosened, but not abandoned, as epistemology has proceeded); that knowledge is something that occurs only cognitively, only in the intellect, in isolation from the emotions and creative impulses; and that knowledge is essentially a matter of one's internal states (that to know something about the external world, for example, is to have an adequate representation, an accurate picture or image of it in the head). All of these claims are conveniently associated in philosophy with the name of Descartes, but they have roots in ancient and medieval thought, and appear in one form or another throughout the modern era.

In art history, criticism, and aesthetics, there is a corresponding set of notions, a set of notions that I have been at pains to describe and criticize already: that art is noncognitive or purely affective (it plays on the emotions rather than the intellect); that art is a matter of *form* rather than content (what makes a work of art good is its "significant form"); that the "fine arts" ought to be distinguished from the crafts and the popular arts; that art is the object of a special sort of experience (aesthetic experience) and a special sort of value (aesthetic value that is unrelated to other human values, for example, moral values); and that art ought to be segregated from the life of the culture into special buildings (museums and concert halls, for example).

Let me say that I believe that all of these claims—both the epistemological and the aesthetic—are false or misleading. Nevertheless, they have exercised a profound influence over the development of our culture, and the results have in many cases been extremely worthwhile. The epistemological claims, for instance, have funded much modern scientific practice. And that practice has been a remarkable success in many ways, at least on its own terms; it has led to a greatly increased understanding and control of the natural world. (This issue will be discussed more thoroughly in the next chapter.) And the modernist picture of the arts, too, has had its astonishing and impressive results, such as the works of Beethoven, Matisse, Martha Graham, and Mies van der Rohe.

But these notions have, as well, proven to be problematic in certain respects. The mechanistic view of the nature and the mania for its control have alienated us from nature and encouraged us in projects that have greatly damaged it. When we account for ourselves as, above all, beings who are capable of intellection, whose highest nature is cognitive rather than physical and affective, we come to feel separated from the order of nature, and justified in exploiting that order. And we have devalued or debased the spiritual traditions of our culture because they did not seem to be well enough justified. This has to some extent set us spiritually adrift, or at least it has set spiritually adrift those people for whom these notions have currency. Likewise, as we have seen, the arts have been alienated from the everyday life of the culture: housed in museums and understood fully only by specialists, great works of art have been separated from everyday interpersonal transactions, and many activities that were before accounted arts (especially the crafts) have been treated as though they were beneath serious intellectual consideration.

We might almost say, in fact, that these epistemological and aesthetic developments are two sides of the same coin, that one is inconceivable without the other. The modern intellectual era, as Dewey declared, is characterized by dualisms: dualisms, for example, between mind and body and between reason and emotion. Whereas knowledge (paradigmatically, science and mathematics) has been associated with reason, art has been associated with emotion. The value that the tradition places on reason has, therefore, led to a concomitant devaluation of art. This is perhaps most clearly expressed in the writings of logical positivists such as A.J. Ayer, by whom expressions of aesthetic judgment are held to be simply expressions of emotion and hence (!) cognitively meaningless.

II

In the course of the *Meditations*, Descartes worked himself into what is known as the "egocentric predicament"; he worked himself into a state where he (claimed to) doubt the existence of anything but his own mind. Whereas the existence of his own mind followed directly from the self-evident fact that he was thinking, the existence of his body and of the external world were (at this stage of the operation) merely unjustifiable assumptions. For all he could prove at this stage, the experiences he was having that were apparently of the external world could be his own dreams, or hallucinations induced by a malicious being. He then proceeded to deduce the existence of his body and the world. (However, this deduction is notoriously flawed.)

There are two things that I want to emphasize about this procedure: first, Descartes asserts that one's knowledge of the external world and even of one's body is of a different sort than knowledge of one's own mental states (in particular, the former is inferred from the latter). Second, Descartes concludes that he is *essentially* a "thing that thinks," and only contingently a thing that moves, or speaks, or interacts with other people.

This procedure, and the picture of what it is to be a human being that emerges from it, is the philosophical construction of a zone of individual isolation. Descartes' method for gaining absolutely certain knowledge is a retreat into himself, which is also a retreat to the foundations of knowledge conceived as incorrigible access to one's own inner states. We come to know the external world, if we come to know it at all, by examining our own "ideas," that is, our own internal representations of that world. And this picture is shared by empiricists such as Hume, for whom knowledge of the external world, if it were possible, could only be arrived at through an examination of internal "sense impressions."

In addition, knowledge is conceived as a matter of knowing *propositions* to be true. Knowing a proposition, in turn, requires a certain sort of relation of that proposition to other propositions known or believed by the agent: a relation of "justification." Knowledge, in a formula accepted in one form or another by almost all epistemologists since the time of Descartes, is justified true belief.[1] That is, for one to know a proposition, the proposition has to be true, one has to believe it to be true, and one has to be in a position to *show* that it is true, or at any rate to give compelling reasons to think that it is true. It is as if the knower were a page on which a list of propositions was inscribed. That the person has other relations to these propositions, and to the real-world situations to which these propositions refer—relations of desire, aversion, interest, indifference, directionality, and interpenetration—is hardly acknowledged. And when it *is* acknowledged, it is regarded as rather an embarrassment. As knowers, as *epistemic* agents, it sometimes seems that we would be better off if we were machines for the manipulation of propositions (computers, for example), rather than the messy organisms we are.

However, the reason that these propositions are not mere syntactical items, mere arrangements of shapes, is that we *reach through* them into the world. We *use* words to refer because we have needs. This is why (so far, anyway) computers can't think: because they can't emote. Our beliefs, that is, are the obscure shadows of our needs; they are means by which a tenuous organism clings to life in a threatening environment. Reference is need.[2] If we ask how it is that my "idea" of a potato can actually refer to a potato in the real world, we cannot answer in terms of the character of the idea. *I* can refer to potatoes because I am a thing that hungers, and a thing into which potatoes can be incorporated. It is the function of our intellects to *meet our needs*. I've *got* to get my body in a position to eat, or have sex, or save my child. That means I've *got* to be detecting what's going on in my environment and responding to it. My logic is an obscure reconstruction of my values. The mind is not a disembodied soul, a computer, or a brain. It is an *organism* in an *environment*.

Furthermore, we use the word 'know' in ordinary language in several ways that are omitted by accounts that focus on propositional knowledge. There is, for example, *knowing how* to do something. This cannot be reduced to propositional knowledge. I can teach my six-year-old daughter many propositions about how to ride a bicycle, but that does not teach her how to ride. That is something that *her body* has to learn. It is an adjustment of body to environment, and of environment to body, not an argumentative structure.[3] Further, we speak of *knowing someone or something*. I know all sorts of propositions about Bill Clinton, but I do not know Bill Clinton. For that, I need to get face to face: I need to be physically present with Clinton. It seems to me that knowing a proposition to be true always depends on knowing how to do things, and on knowing people and things. If I did not know how to do anything, and furthermore didn't know anyone, I would never come to know the truth of any propositions at all. So in fact, these other notions are fundamental. Here again, the modernist legacy is one of artificial isolation.

An analogous process of isolation has taken place in the arts. As we have discussed, the ancient Greek word *technē* and its Latin cousin *ars* traditionally refer to the *way* something is made, rather than to the object made. To do something with art was to do it with great skill. Fundamentally, the term connoted craft, or the devoted and skilled use of materials for a satisfying and practical result. That was indeed the way such arts as painting, sculpture, and architecture were conceived through the renaissance, and most of the great practitioners of these arts were members of crafts guilds. Such arts were not pursued simply in order to make beautiful or aesthetically challenging objects, but for religious rite or festive occasion. (Indeed, this is also the function of the arts in most non-Western cultures.)

To repeat myself with a twist: in the eighteenth century, in response to such developments as a growing middle class and increased secularization of culture, the notion of the "fine arts" was developed. This notion is characterized by the claim that works of art have no practical purpose, and that they are precisely to be contrasted with, rather than integrated into, the everyday life of the culture. Works of art are the objects, in addition, of a particular mode of human experience—"aesthetic" experience—which is to be characterized, again, in terms of "disinterested pleasure" or "psychical distance." That is, works of art do not, or at any rate should not, play any role in what Bullough quaintly terms our "practical, actual lives" (as if we also, somewhere else perhaps, simultaneously led impractical, nonactual lives). The aesthetic experience is not an expression of, say, sexual or economic desire, but is a pure appreciation of pure form. Works of art, hence, have no cognitive content, or they ought to be treated as if they had no cognitive content.

This gives rise to a situation in which art is simply regarded as a luxury, something with no practical value. Art is not something we *need*, but only something we desire as a rewarding occasion for nonpractical cultivation of taste. And art is something that is done, or done really well, only by (slightly crazed) specialists.

III

Though I think the modernist picture of human knowledge is false to the core, and though I think it can be *shown* to be false, I want to emphasize a common-sense objection. First of all, we all know perfectly well that we are creatures who are embedded in an external world: a world of trees, cars, other people, and so forth. So there is no point, for present purposes, in trying to prove that. Second, we all know that we are *participants* in, and not merely spectators of, this world; we know that we alter our environment and that our environment alters us. I suggest that this is absolutely key in formulating a defensible epistemology. Third, though this is no argument against the modernist picture, it is worth pointing out that it is historically exhausted, that philosophers from Dewey and Heidegger to Rorty and Foucault have been busily showing us the bankruptcy of this picture for a hundred years.

As against the modernist conception of human experience—on which, to repeat, to experience the external world is to examine one's internal representations, as if one was watching a movie—we need to develop a conception in which experience is a dynamic participation in existence. We need to emphasize the *situatedness* of the subject in time and space and within a social context. Such an expanded notion of human situation is developed beautifully in Arnold Berleant's *The Aesthetics of Environment*:

> This, then, is what environment is; this is what environment *means*: a fusion of organic awareness, of meanings both conscious and unaware, of geographical location, of physical presence, personal time, pervasive movement. There is no outward view, no distant scene. There are no surroundings separate from my presence in that place.[4]

I shall return to this notion of 'fusion' between person and situation presently. But notice that the modernist conception is related to dualism, the notion that mind and body are two radically distinct sorts of thing. This is not compatible with what we know about animals such as we are; it is not compatible with a naturalistic approach to what it is to be a human being. People are of the order of nature, are always in the process of trying to achieve a mutual adaptation of organism and environment. That situation is a participation in, or perhaps more deeply, an identification with, the world.

Indeed, it is worth pointing out that the distinction of the organism from the environment is itself only a convenience, and is, in any case, fluid. We absorb parts of the environment into ourselves, and eliminate parts of ourselves into the environment. As we move through the environment, the environment, quite literally, moves through us. The materials out of which we are composed, and into which we impress our mark (out of which we construct shelter, for example) *are* the environment in transformation. And in social life, persons are parts, at times overwhelmingly important parts, of the environment of one another. I suggest that it is our complete embeddedness in the environment that makes human knowledge possible, and that we need to articulate a new orientation in epistemology that is true to our *identity* with the world.[5]

Such an orientation would be new in some sense to the west, but it is the traditional conception of knowledge in India. The closest Sanskrit equivalent to the English term 'philosophy' is *darśana*. *Darśana* is not spectation, but *realization*; to know an object is to become one with it, to realize it in oneself, as a computer realizes a program. Radhakrishnan writes:

> To know reality one must have an actual experience of it. One does not merely *know* the truth in Indian philosophy; one *realizes* it. To see [*dṛś*, the root of *darśana*] is to have direct intuitive experience of the object, or, rather, to realize it in the sense of becoming one with it. No complete knowledge is possible as long as there is a relationship of the subject on one hand and the object on the other.[6]

Indeed, the King James Bible uses "know" to mean "have sex with," a usage that reveals something deep about knowledge. To know is to interpenetrate with someone or something out of desire. Knowing is much more like having sex than like watching a movie.

Elsewhere, I have tried to construct such an epistemology using the notion of *fusion*.[7] 'Fusion,' as I use it, is a technical term describing certain relations. Technicalities aside, the central notion is this: to experience the world is not to enter a certain internal state. It is not to entertain, say, a certain mental image or representation which turns out to represent the world accurately. There *is* no purely internal state in virtue of which I experience the world, and which is necessary for me to have the experience of the world I am having. Experience is a dynamic *transaction* with the world; experience, as it were, occurs *between* myself and my environment, or rather arises in the interaction of myself and my environment. I am a physical object among other physical objects, and vision, hearing, and the other sense modalities are ways that physical objects have of bumping into each other. To see a tree is to be fused with a tree in this sense. Seeing is like breathing: a process in which part of my environment is incorporated into my body, in which the distinction between myself and the object is collapsed.

And here again, we are pursuing a structure of thought which has recurred throughout this book. We are *already* fused with our environment; we are already things among other things; this is already the source of any knowledge we possess. It is not a matter of ceasing to be spectators of the world; it is a

matter of realizing that we never were, and never can be spectators. To be a spectator is to be safe. No one has ever been
eaten by a movie monster. We seek safety by pretending that
we can experience the world at a distance. But the world is all
around us and inside us; the world *is* us. There is no escape, no
evasion, no surcease. Modern epistemology, like modern
painting, perhaps, arises in part out of fear and hatred for the
world; a new epistemology and a new art might arise out of
joy in the world even in the face of cruelty and danger.

Knowledge supervenes, typically, on experience. For
human subjects, a dynamic interchange with the environment
yields a series of beliefs. If these beliefs are true, they constitute
knowledge. Think here of scientific experimentation. The scientist systematically (or haphazardly, for that matter) creates
changes in the environment and experiences the result. Scientific experimentation is a transaction in which the scientist
alters the environment and is in turn altered by the environment in the sense that the experiment effects knowledge, as
Dewey saw with clarity in *The Quest for Certainty*. And as he
also saw, the dream of absolute certainty is an illusion born of
fear; belief acquired in interchange with the environment is
always open to revision under further interchange. But knowledge is the result of an active construction within the environment.

This is particularly clear with regard to non-propositional
knowledge. To know how to ride a bicycle, I must actually get
on a bicycle and ride. In fact, I first have to get on a bicycle and
fall down; gradually, I "get the feel of it," something that can
only be accomplished in practical, and risky, life-experience.
"Know-how," as we call it, is a practical affair; it is knowledge
that can *only* arise in a full-scale integration with the environment, as for the cyclist the bicycle is an extension of the body.
And I can get to know *you* only by interacting with you, only
transactionally. I need to see something of your emotion,
something of what you need, and what you reject; it will not
help me very much to hear you reel off a list of propositions.
In turn, my knowledge of you is a *feel* for you, rather than
something propositional.

Likewise, I believe that the modernist conception of art is false and invidious. First of all, no human activity can be truly nonpractical in the way the modernist myth directs. When it comes time for people to make things or look at things or listen to things, they cannot leave the normal range of human desires behind. I might go to the museum to impress my friends or relax after a hard day; one way or another, if I go at all, I go with a human purpose. And when I see a picture, for example, of a nude person or a serene landscape, I respond not, or not only, to the pure form—the combination of lines and colors—but also to what is depicted. And this response is an engagement rather than a disengagement of desire. Art, in other words, emerges from and fulfills real human needs.

And as we have seen, even as the "fine arts" are segregated from the life of the culture, the full range of what are traditionally accounted arts—the crafts, the popular arts (such as blues and country music)—are all the while just as fundamental to the life of the culture as ever. If we are willing to countenance such activities as art, then the everyday life of the culture remains permeated with art. Mara Miller, in her book *The Garden as an Art*, points out that the garden has been regarded as an art for most of Western history, and is so regarded even today in Japanese culture, for example. And she points out also that regarding the garden as art is not compatible with "aesthetic distance":

> What does it mean for a work of art to be also a site? What are the implications of this for the garden as a work of art?
>
> For one thing, we enter it. It is spatially and temporally continuous with the rest of the world in which we live. There is no change of scale. Psychic distance is severely challenged, as physical distance is literally destroyed. We do not merely look at the garden, we are surrounded by it, bringing the same psychological habits of perception to the garden that we bring to any other environment. In addition, the tempo of our experience of the garden is the same as that of ordinary life.

To the extent that special tempi may be called for, we ourselves initiate the change, as we do in our normal environment, rather than respond to changes initiated externally, as we do in listening to music or watching a film or drama.[8]

Indeed, many folks devote to their gardens the sort of absorbed activity that I have describing as art. But the nature of the garden involves the slow mutual adaptation of organism and environment that is, in germ, human existence in the world. Recovery of the arthood of gardens is, hence, recovery of art outside the modernist myth, and recovery of ourselves in our fusion with the world.

As I have said, I would like to regard art as a way of doing. We are engaged in art when we are performing some activity for its own sake as well as for the sake of whatever end may be in view. And the results of such activities, if they give rise to objects which are themselves of a sort that are inherently satisfying to use for their ends, are works of art. So the experience of a painting may be inherently satisfying, as well as a needed relaxation or a challenging conceptual exercise.

The fundamental experience of art, as I said in the first chapter, is an experience of *absorption*. Notice that the notions of absorption and fusion are closely related: to become absorbed in something is to become fused with it. Ben-Ami Scharfstein, in his book *Birds, Beasts, and Other Artists*, which is the best recent book in aesthetics that I know, writes that "all art . . . expresses the need of the individual to live beyond himself."[9] And he also says that "art is the attempt to remain individual in expression while merging or fusing with what is beyond the individual" (p. 208). Art is, thus, a simultaneous expansion and annihilation of the self, and in both aspects is at once exhilerating and dangerous. As has already been indicated, art can be regarded as a form of fusion that invites us into other forms of fusion. Art involves fusion with materials: absorption in the process of working. And art's fusion opens from that into other fusions; art is fused experience that invites us into fusion within ourselves, fusion with one another, fusion with the world, and fusion with the divine. I want to distinguish the varieties of fusion according to their objects, according to that with which the individual becomes fused. And I want to assert that it is the characteristic function of art to achieve fusion in all these dimensions.

First of all, there is *intrapersonal* fusion, that is, an integration of the capacities and faculties of a single person. Art, I claim, typically effects such an integration. When one is engaged in art, either as a maker or an experiencer, many of one's faculties—emotional, cognitive, physical—are called into play simultaneously. This is, in part, what makes the activity autotelic; one has the sensation that one is being *made whole* in the activity itself, an experience that is inherently satisfying. In fact, I think that this is what characteristically leads to what we regard as masterpieces of art; in them, the intellectual and the emotional are exquisitely balanced, and embodied in a made object. Intrapersonal fusion, however, if the epistemological view put forward here is right, cannot merely be an internal operation. One becomes fused, becomes a coherent personality, only in interaction with the environment. So this aspect of fusion, like the others, is separated only for convenience; fusion with the environment *is*, in many ways, fusion with the self.

Fusion of the person with the environment, is perhaps the dimension of fusion that I have emphasized most so far; it includes the absorption of the artist in her materials, and the absorption of the viewer in the work of art. In both cases, one experiences a "loss of self." And I want to interpret that phrase quite literally as the absorption of oneself into the 'external' object. Through the loss of self one achieves the expansion of self: as one becomes identified with what surrounds one, one encompasses it even as it encompasses one. This is typified, for instance, by, for example, the medicine bundles of the Menominee tribe. The Menominee place tokens of various animals into a bundle, with the result that the bundle-holder becomes fused with that animal; one gains, for example, the hunting prowess and ferocity of a mink. (I will return to this example in the next chapter.) The bundle "represents" animals in the service of self-identification, and for practical purposes. But like the bundle charms of the African Kongo region, which are intended for healing or attack, they are made with devotion and are, closed or open, beautiful.

Third, there is *interpersonal* fusion. This, I take it, is again a central and characteristic feature of the making and experiencing of works of art. It can be as mundane as the attempt to be understood as one writes a poem, or as ecstatic as a festival in which one's sense of individuality is emptied into a collective activity and consciousness. Think, for example, of a punk show, in which the slam-dancing audience becomes a single organism moving in waves to the music. Indeed, much art of much of the world is made and deployed in social and festive contexts. Think again here of the tea ceremony. Navajo "sings" for example, though they have practical purposes such as healing, incorporate many of the arts (story-telling, music, and sand-painting, for example) into a context that is a creation and affirmation of a culture, and of the individual's place within that culture. And the same might be said, for example, of two-step country and Western dancing. As one performs a line dance, the agent of the action becomes the group, acting both spontaneously and with perfect coordination. What music one listens to, what visual art one enjoys, how one adorns oneself, and so forth: all these are artistic means of expressing cultural identification.

Finally, art may achieve cosmic or spiritual fusion with the divine (if any) or even with the universe as a whole. This is surely in some sense the goal of religious art of all sorts. Christian art of the middle ages, for example, is an attempt to depict the divine realm, to make it sensible, that is, to bring it together with the world in which we live. Though I am not currently interested in evaluating whether there is any truth in this purported function of art, I want to point out that most of the world's great art has been made for such purposes. And in fact all these dimensions of fusion are themselves fused. People in a festival, for example, may be employing objects they have shaped in a culturally significant way to achieve fusion with their gods.

IV

If we identify fusion as the source of our knowledge about the world and one another, and if we identify art as a source of fusion of a particularly intense and systematic sort, then it follows that art is an important source and paradigm of knowledge. This is precisely what is denied by the modernist picture, with its consignment of art to the realm of the "emotive." But one thing that we have been experiencing here is the collapse of the distinction between the emotive and the cognitive. We come to know because we are in a certain situation, and we retain our knowledge because we are moved and changed in certain ways by that situation. In these processes, emotion and cognition operate simultaneously, or rather they are distinguishable only as moments embedded in the total experience.

It is by the manipulation of materials that we come to know those materials, that is, to know a part of our world, and this is also how we come to know how to do various things with materials. That is, knowledge is, paradigmatically, the skilled making that is the primordial meaning of 'art.' And of course: in this process, we also come to know various propositions, for example, those embodying procedures for the further development of skills. We come to be able to *describe*, say, clay, and the vessel made of clay, with a depth and an appreciation that only arises in thorough and involving experience. And this in turn ramifies into our experience of the vessel thus made, and of similar vessels: as we understand more, our experience of use is enriched. Indeed, the experience of making a vessel may lead to a cherishing of vessels and their makers, an understanding of and respect for persons and things that could not arise by other means.

Think, as well, about how we in fact come to learn about our own cultures and about what it means to be a member of our culture. We learn this by *participation* in shared rites and celebrations, in collaborative works of art. That is, we learn it by an experience of fusion among members of our culture, as at parades, football games, musical performances, classrooms. And with regard to other cultures: it is one thing to master a set of propositions about them and quite another to meet them face to face, to be confronted by their people and their art. It is in the possibility of *that* fusion that multi-cultural understanding might be realized.

Finally, think about how we learn about *ourselves*, learn who we are and what we are capable of doing. First of all, we learn this in all the ways mentioned above: we construct ourselves, or find out how we are constructed, as we engage in our cultures and with our world: always by active participation, artistic participation, rather than by passive reception. It is often held that one finds out about oneself by introspection, by retreating into oneself to explore the inner terrain. In general, however, I cannot come to know my own capacities without employing my capacities in the world; I cannot know my potential without beginning to realize it externally; I cannot know what I love doing without doing things. All of this is at once a gathering of knowledge about the world and about oneself. And it can be profitably understood on the model of art. You cannot find out what you love doing by simply going out and running through a set of activities. You have to *let* yourself love, allow yourself to become entrapped in the activity itself. Love is not something you *make* happen, but something you *allow* to happen in an absorption in an activity (or, for that matter, in a person).

V

The reader will, at this point, hardly be surprised to find that this conception of knowing as an art, and of art as a fundamental source of knowledge, requires a deep re-envisioning of the aims and practices of education.

The model of education suggested by the modernist picture is one in which the student is a passive and passionless absorber of propositions. Recall that on this picture, knowledge is propositional, and that justification (which is held to be necessary for knowledge) is a feature of the evidential relations obtaining between propositions. So if a teacher can, as it were, inscribe the right set of propositions on the *tabula rasa* of the student, the teacher has imparted knowledge. The deepest and most obvious impulse that children have is to interact actively and physically with the environment. But we try to make them sit still as we lecture to them, or as they memorize or copy propositions out of books. The impulse to *move* is itself a *demand* for knowledge; it is an impulse for exploration of and fusion with the environment, and hence of and with the child's own capacities. Dance and sport, as concerted forms of movement, are ways of knowing.

Note, as one symptom of the modernist conception of education, the way that the results of education are measured in America: by standardized tests. These simply attempt to assess whether the student has memorized the desired propositions. To say that this process is a dehumanization of education is an understatement. By the standards deployed in the SAT, the computer that grades the exam is more knowledgeable than the people who take it. Notice, however, that the computer knows nothing whatever. That in itself ought to indicate that the models of knowledge and of education in play here are radically impoverished. And I hope it is clear by now that such tests could not possibly measure knowledge in its richest sense. Try to imagine a multiple-choice test for art, for example.

It is hardly surprising that this picture makes the arts peripheral to education. Whereas the arts consist of active exploration and administration of materials and states of affairs, our goal is the inscription of propositions. The segregation of art as an emotive luxury item in our culture immediately renders the arts superfluous to our educational aims. And indeed, when school budgets are trimmed, it is often arts education that is lopped off first.

I have argued that knowledge is always a result of a transaction between persons and environments, that knowledge always is a feature of the *situation* in which both the knower and the known are embedded. It follows, I think, that the most effective means of education is to engage the student as actively as possible in as wide as possible a variety of situations. The arts are precisely a systematic range of situations in which people can be embedded, and they are the sorts of situations most elaborately developed as sources of knowledge. Over many centuries, we have found that some materials are particularly fascinating to work, and, worked, are particularly satisfying to employ in a range of capacities. We have dubbed these processes 'arts.' And, again over a period of centuries, we have labored to understand how best to employ these materials in these capacities. Thus, the arts form a body of cultural tradition for teaching, a set of resources for the focused achievement of fusion, and, hence, knowledge.

Note, too, that these particular materials and processes have come to be accounted arts because they are particularly suited to give rise to activities that can be pursued for their own sake as well as for the sake of an end. Thus if you teach a child to paint or to make music, you may well find it more difficult to stop than to start her, particularly if you allow her to paint or play what she wants. The structure of motivation in present-day American education is absurdly teleological; we educate people to "grow the economy," "achieve competitiveness in the global marketplace," "develop human resources." That such ends are incapable of motivating students is too obvious to need emphasis. In fact, it is absurd to think that such goals could motivate *anyone* to do *anything*. After all, whatever I do, its effect on American global competitiveness is less than negligible.

But the arts are the arts precisely because they spontaneously generate a structure of motivation. They provide the motivation to pursue the activity *from within the character of the activity itself*. Furthermore, they make use of the fundamental human impulse to explore and transform the environment in inherently satisfying ways. Perhaps the most profound change that would be achieved by centralizing the arts as a model and a method for education is that this would provide a fundamental shift in the pursuit of educational ends. This also holds out the possibility of unlocking the creativity of students, of allowing them to find what they love doing and what they can do best. Ironically enough, that is itself likely to increase "productivity."

Here, however, we also see the possibility of achieving a profound *moral* transformation in how students are regarded and treated in the educational setting. For when we attempt to imprint propositions on people in order to develop them as economic resources, we are using these people as mere means to achieve an extrinsic goal. We are treating them as if they were so much bauxite awaiting technological development. Indeed, this picture is often accompanied by the ever-increasing demand for more technology in the classroom, as if machines could educate people where people cannot. There is nothing wrong with technology in the classroom (indeed, the arts themselves, as we shall see, are technologies in the oldest sense), but looking at the classroom itself as a technology for the processing of raw materials into valuable human resources is both educationally counter-productive and dehumanizing.

So the final suggestion is this: that the activity of teaching itself can be understood as an art, or transformed into an art. One teaches, when one teaches as an art, for the sake of teaching itself, and in devotion to the students for their own sake as human beings, rather than merely as resources to be developed for yet other ends. Indeed, I believe that most teachers embarked on careers in teaching for just such reasons, because the activity is inherently satisfying. Yet the technological picture of the classroom that has resulted from the modernist picture of art and knowledge forces teachers to aim at some end without regard to the means. Teaching, like art and knowledge, is an experience of fusion, and teaching, like art and knowledge at their epiphanic moments, is a fusion in love.

Notes

1. I have criticized this conception of knowledge in detail in two papers: "Knowledge is Merely True Belief," *American Philosophical Quarterly* vol. 28, no. 2 (April 1991). "Why Knowledge is Merely True Belief," *The Journal of Philosophy*, vol. 89, no. 4 (April 1992).

2. I intend to defend this position elaborately elsewhere.

3. See Gilbert Ryle, *The Concept of Mind* (London: Hutchinson House, 1949), chapter II.

4. Arnold Berleant, *The Aesthetics of Environment* (Philadelphia: Temple University Press, 1992), 34.

5. I attempt to set out such a view in my paper "Radical Externalism About Experience," *Philosophical Studies* (forthcoming).

6. *A Sourcebook of Indian Philosophy*, xxv–vi.

7. "Radical Externalism."

8. Mara Miller, *The Garden as an Art* (Albany, NY: State University of New York Press, 1993), 102, 103.

9. Ben-Ami Scharfstein, *Of Birds, Beasts, and Other Artists* (New York: New York University Press, 1988), 213.

Chapter 7

The Tao of Technology

One of the deepest problems in Western education, then, is its technological orientation. We regard persons as resources and schools as processing plants. The solutions proposed for the deep problems of pedagogy consist, often, simply of technological improvements. And of course, the "problem" of technology is both more pervasive and more destructive than simply a misguided strategy of teaching. In this chapter, I want to explore the problem of technology, in particular as it is formulated by Heidegger in the seminal essay "The Question Concerning Technology," in relation to the aesthetics of the ordinary.

We of the West have for a long time been learning to experience technology as a problem. The most obvious symptoms of this problem are the destruction of the environment and the dehumanization of persons. We have, it seems, come to regard nature, and one another, as *resources*, as stuff to be exploited, as, in Heidegger's phrase, "standing reserve." In one sense, 'technology' simply picks out the artifacts by which we try to manipulate our environment: machinery, for example. But in a deeper sense, the sense in which I will use it here, 'technology' refers to the complicated and interwoven set of beliefs and attitudes that give us to think that we can and should manipulate our environment, and which, hence, transform the environment into something to be manipulated, as well as into instrumentation.

Indeed, the environmental movement itself, though in its extreme moments it condemns technology altogether, and though it always has suspicions toward technology, often sets itself up in a technological relation to the world, and to technology. It regards technology precisely as a threat to resources, that is, to technology itself; it criticizes technology for consuming rather than accumulating a standing reserve. We should fight to preserve the rain forests, for example, because they harbor as yet unexploited medicinal plants, or because we are releasing too much carbon dioxide and too little oxygen. And the resolution proposed to the problem of technology is itself technological: the creation, say, of machines to clean up the products of other machines.

The resolution is technological, too, in a deeper sense. Heidegger writes:

> [M]odern technology too is a means to an end. That is why the instrumental conception of technology conditions every attempt to bring man into the right relation to technology. Everything depends on our manipulating technology in the proper manner as a means. We will, as we say, "get" technology "spiritually in hand." We will master it. The will to mastery becomes all the more urgent as technology threatens to slip from human control.[1]

In other words, the way we conceive technology, as conditioned by an instrumental conception of means and ends, is the way we conceive technology as a whole in relation to ourselves, and the way we conceive ourselves in relation to technology as a whole. And as Heidegger implies, technology is at its most intense precisely when we come to reject it, because at that point the demand for a forcible transformation of the world is at its most importunate.

Thus, the "problem" of technology becomes something that is *in principle* impossible to evade or resolve; technology as a way of thinking and being in the world becomes for us something in which we are necessarily embedded in virtue of our cultural situation. To conceive of technology as a problem (which is just the way I conceived it in relation to education) is to conceive it technologically. To reject technology is precisely to embrace it with particular fervor. If technology has made a mess of our planet, we need more technology to clean it up. But here we do not question the central commitments of *thinking* technologically: the treatment of the world as an object over against us subjects (what will be discussed in a moment as the structure of representation), and the treatment of the use of this object as means to achieve our subjective ends.

I

I am going to offer a "solution" to the "problem" of technology, a solution which I draw from the ancient texts of Chinese Taoism, and which is in some respects Heideggerian in spirit. The solution is this: there is no solution. We are not going to *transform* technology into something we could come to regard as wholesome, and we are not going to transform ourselves away from technological thinking. These things are inescapable. Or perhaps the matter should be put this way: any *attempt* to escape them only ensnares us in them more thoroughly. So what I am claiming amounts to this: we ought to stop trying to evade or escape technology; we should see if we cannot find *acceptance* of the fact that technology is what we do and how we think.

If we could stop trying to transform technology, we would have transformed technology once and for all. For example, if we could enjoy technology for its own sake (and we ought to admit that we often do!), then we would have transformed mere instrumentality into an artistic devotion to means. There is only one way to enter into a nontechnological relation to technology: simply to abide with satisfaction within technology itself. To do this would be to transform our relationship to ourselves and our world by renouncing transformation. Heidegger writes: "when we once open ourselves expressly to the *essence* of technology we find ourselves unexpectedly taken into a freeing claim" (304). We will return to the notion of the essence of technology in a moment, but for now it should be noted that the problem with this is just that it is (apparently, at any rate) impossible, or at least impossible as a *solution* to the problem of technology. For it means that we need to *give up* our goal in order to achieve it, or rather, give up goals in general in order to achieve a specific goal. Better yet: we need to give up even giving up. That is, we need to hold on to our goals, which after all are *our* goals, and also transform our relation to the means of achieving them, simply by becoming present in them, simply by acknowledging what is already the case. (The earlier discussion of the *Gītā* ought to resonate here.) This structure of thought is worthy of exploration, if only because technology lurks in every other available structure. (Of course, the question of whether this structure *is* available is open.)

Here is a quotation from *Tao Te Ching* that embodies the suggestion I am putting forward:

> Do you think you can take over the universe
>   and improve it?
> I do not think it can be done.
>
> The universe is sacred.
> You cannot improve it.
> If you try to change it, you will ruin it.
> If you try to hold it, you will lose it.[2]

This passage renounces programs to reform people or culture or the world. And because of passages such as this, Taoism is often thought of as antitechnological. But notice: though technology emerges from, or rather is, the attitude that we can take over the world and improve it, technology is itself now part of the world. So now it is part of what cannot be improved, of what must be embraced. If you try to change *technology*, you will ruin the world.

A central concept in Taoism is *wu wei*, which can be translated as "non-doing" or "doing nothing." And in spoken Chinese, the phrase could also mean "non-becoming," "no artifice," "no power," or "speechlessness." (These phrases employ different characters, all of which are pronounced "wei.") So

Taoism seems to recommend doing nothing, saying nothing, becoming nothing, abjuring power: "The sage goes about doing nothing, teaching no-talking" (*Tao Te Ching*, chapter 2).

In fact, however (and this topic is one of the most deeply explored in Chinese philosophy), *wu wei* is not inaction, but action which is harmonious with the way things are, action done as part of the universe. It is action, or rather movement (since action, as implying agency, is precisely what is at stake) of a thing among other things. The Taoist sage does not cease moving, speaking, building, becoming, but he moves as water moves, speaks as the wind speaks, builds as mountains are built. Becoming is achieved through and in him, but not by him. The sage *goes about* doing nothing, and *speaks* no-talking.

This way of doing is summarized in a great passage from the *Chuang Tzu*:

> Confucius was seeing the sights at Lü-liang, where the water falls from a height of thirty fathoms and races and boils along for forty li, so swift that no fish or other water creature can swim in it. He saw a man dive into the water and, supposing that the man was in some trouble and desired to end his life, he ordered his disciples to line up on the bank and pull the man out. But after the man had gone a couple of hundred paces, he came out of the water and began strolling along the base of the embankment, his hair streaming down, singing a song. Confucius ran after him and said, "At first I thought you were a ghost, but now I see you're a man. May I ask if you have some special way of staying afloat in the water?"
>
> "I have no way. I began with what I was used to, grew up with my nature, and let things come to completion with fate. I go under with the swirls and come out with the eddies, following along the way the water goes and never thinking about myself. That's how I stay afloat."[3]

The image of this man simply allowing himself to be borne along by the water is an image of the Taoist sage simply allowing himself to borne along by what is. And his attitude goes further than acceptance; as his hair streams and he sings, he gives himself over to a pleasure in the way things are, a joy even in danger. And despite the fact that "Tao" is usually translated as "The Way," this Taoist sage says that he has no way. Indeed, that is Taoism in its deepest depth. Taoism is a way that has given up ways, a way that is a sheer opening, an allowance to be, a grateful largesse.

Is this antitechnological? Is acceptance of the world as it is and the abjuration of agency and way something we could *pit against* technology, or into which we might transform technology? Well, it is not itself technological, though it could be performed as a technological program of self and world-transformation (precisely then, though, it could never be achieved). But picture how *wu wei* would play out if the Taoist sage were to find herself in a situation in which technology were already in place, in which the technological transformation of the environment were underway and technological thinking inescapable. In such a situation, the technology in the world and in the self would have to be accepted. The Taoist sage in a technological culture simply accepts technology and lives within it gratefully. But that puts the sage in a non-technological relation to technology, in which technology in coming to appear is transformed.

Or perhaps as Heidegger would put it, to enter into *wu wei* with regard to technology would be to allow technology to emerge in its essence. It is not quite accurate to say that, within Taoism, we *ought* to act as a thing among other things, that we ought to *abjure* agency. Rather, when we act, we *always do* act as a thing among other things. That is, *we already have what we want*; we are all already sages. (It is a commonplace of Buddhism that we are all already Buddhas.) Heidegger writes:

> Wherever a man opens his eyes and ears, unlocks his heart and gives himself over to meditating and striving, shaping and working, entreating and thanking, he

finds himself everywhere already brought into the unconcealed. The unconcealment of the unconcealed has already come to pass whenever it calls man forth into the modes of revealing allotted to him. When man, in his way, from within unconcealment reveals that which presences, he merely responds to the call of unconcealment even when he contradicts it. (p. 300)

Here Heidegger treats the essence of technology as a *poiēsis*: a bringing-forth. And in virtue of our participation in technology, we already participate in this bringing-forth that lies at technology's heart. Heidegger draws a distinction between the correct view about technology and the truth about technology. So far, I have been discussing the former. But the essence of technology is precisely a *poiēsis*, a bringing-forth (p. 293). Even more specifically, it is a *physis*, "the arising of something out of itself" (p. 293). The truth of technology is that *we* arise out of ourselves within it, as through it we give rise to things. Or: in its essence, technology is not a way we bring things about, but a way in which things bring themselves about through us and in us. Technology, conceived nontechnologically, is simply an example of the way things come to pass, not a grand tribute to the power of human agency.

Kuo Hsiang, in a marvelous ancient commentary on *The Chuang Tzu*, puts very much the same point like this:

The music of nature is not an entity existing outside of things. . . . Such non-being is non-being, it cannot produce being. Before being itself is introduced, it cannot produce beings. Then by whom are things produced? They spontaneously produce themselves, that is all. By this is not meant that there is an "I" to produce. The "I" cannot produce things and things cannot produce the "I." The "I" is self-existent [spontaneously produces itself]. Because it is so by itself, we call it natural. Everything is what it is through nature and not by taking any action.[4]

Notice that Kuo Hsiang does not issue a *denial* of human agency and identity. He simply identifies human identity with the identity of all other things, and human production with the production of all other things. Applied to technology as a mode of human production, that would be the experience of technology in its essence.

To enter into a nontechnological relation to technology, or rather, to see that we are *already* in a nontechnological relation to technology, will lead us into a reconstrual of means/ends relations. To find the essence of technology in the spontaneous self-creation of things will lead us into a different understanding of causality, something which is surely occurring both in Kuo Hsiang and in Heidegger.

Here, though, I want to emphasize Kuo Hsiang's radical envisioning of the "I," of the "human subject." The "I" can neither be produced, nor can it produce anything. Our agency neither emerges out of things, nor do things emerge out of our agency. (And it is worth noting that things are also not produced by divine agency, for Kuo Hsiang: the universe itself is not a manufactured item.) *Wu wei* must then be construed not as a renunciation of action, but as a realization of the illusoriness of action, of one's embeddedness in a world of *physis*, a world spontaneously producing itself, both in the movement of tectonic plates and in production of factories. And we are ourselves being spontaneously produced. As Heidegger says:

> Since man drives technology forward, he takes part in ordering as a way of revealing. But the unconcealment itself, within which ordering unfolds, is never human handiwork, any more than is the realm man traverses every time he as a subject relates to an object. (p. 300)

Technology as unconcealment is something that happens in us and to some extent through us, but it is not something we *do*.

Here again is the *Chuang Tzu*:

> The K'uei [a one-legged creature] said to the millipede, "I have this one leg that I hop along on, though I make

little progress. Now how in the world do you manage
to work all those ten thousand legs of yours?"

The millipede said, "You don't understand.
Haven't you ever watched a man spit? He just gives a
hawk and out it comes, some drops as big as pearls,
some as fine as mist, raining down in a jumble of
countless particles. Now all I do is put in motion the
natural mechanism in me—I'm not aware of how the
thing works." (p. 104)

From a certain point of view, spitting is beautiful; a bejeweled
and extremely elaborate spray, like the spray of the ocean. But
one could not achieve any certain beautiful pattern of spit
through intending to do so; any particular beautiful pattern
that is achieved is simply something that one allows the natural mechanism to accomplish. Perhaps, the Taoists hint, all
human action, including that which we are pleased to call
intentional, is of this nature. Perhaps everything that "we do"
is in fact something that we allow the natural mechanism to
achieve.

II

Heidegger hints that there is a way of making, or of allowing
things to come to appearance, that still lies at technology's
essence, and which might still enable us to think technology
nontechnologically. This way of making is art. Heidegger
writes:

There was a time when it was not technology alone
that bore the name *techne*. Once that revealing which
brings forth truth into the splendor of radiant appearance was also called *techne*.

Once there was a time when the bringing forth of
the true into the beautiful was called *techne*. The
poiesis of the fine arts was also called *techne*.

At the outset of the destining of the West, in
Greece, the arts soared to the supreme height of the

revealing granted them. They illuminated the presence [*Gegenwart*] of the gods and the dialogue of divine and human destinings. And art was simply called *technē*. It was a single, manifold revealing. It was pious, *promos*, i.e., yielding to the holding sway and safekeeping of truth.

The arts were not derived from the artistic. Art works were not enjoyed aesthetically. Art was not a sector of cultural activity. (pp. 315, 316)

It is odd for us to think that art might lie at the origin and at the heart of technology. For in our parlance, art and technology are precisely opposed. No opposition runs more deeply through modernity than the opposition between degrading, dehumanizing industrial production—the role of the assembly-line worker, for example—and the exalted creativity of the great artist.

Indeed, the way we conceive art is itself governed by a technological treatment of technology. This conception corresponds in its rise, and perhaps in its current decline, with the industrial revolution. This conception includes, above all, a distinction of art from other forms of human making: a distinction of it from the craft and skill which still resonate in *technē*, and from mechanical or industrial mass-production. Heidegger suggests that these modes of human production share deeper similarities than their conceptualization within the Western tradition suggests. They share, for example, an origin.

In China, the concept of *shu* or skill, which has certainly been translated into English as 'art,' has resisted, or has never been subject to, these particular transformations. Chinese art has maintained its connection to piety, or at any rate, to deep beliefs, especially Taoist beliefs. For another, skill and creativity have not been firmly distinguished. Here is a passage from *The Chuang Tzu*, which expresses very clearly a Taoist conception of skill:

Woodworker Ch'ing carved a piece of wood and made a bell stand, and when it was finished, everyone who saw it marveled, for it seemed to be the work of gods or spirits. When the marquis of Lu saw it, he asked, "What art is it you have?"

Ch'ing replied, "I am only a craftsman—how would I have any art? There is one thing, however. When I am going to make a bell stand, I never let it wear out my energy. I always fast in order to still my mind. When I have fasted for three days, I no longer have any thought of congratulations or rewards, of titles or stipends. When I have fasted for five days, I no longer have any thought of praise or blame, of skill or clumsiness. And when I have fasted for seven days, I am so still that I forget I have four limbs and a form and a body. By this time, the ruler and his court no longer exist for me. My skill is concentrated and all outside distractions fade away. After that, I go into the mountain forest and examine the natural form of the trees. If I find one of superlative form, and I can see a bell stand there, I put my hand to the job of carving; if not, I let it go. That way, I am simply matching my nature with the nature of the tree. (pp. 205, 206, translation altered a bit)

Ch'ing is not, at least by his own account, the creator of the bell stand. He is simply, as it were, an occasion for letting the bell stand emerge. He identifies himself with things in a "spiritual" or "devotional" process, and then he allows things to create themselves, to undergo *physis*. And as he does so, he is also in the process of allowing himself to create himself, or allowing things to constitute him as a maker of bell stands; that is, his *poiēsis* is his *physis*, and his *physis* is the *physis* of bell stands.

III

Notice that the technological conception of technology requires an ontological gap between agents and that upon which they act, between the "mind" and the inanimate material to be transformed. This is the structure of being that Heidegger refers to as "enframing": treating the world as an object. And notice, too, that this "enframing" is perfectly exemplified in the representational structure of Western art into this century. One *comprehends* the object in the picture, or by making the picture; one exerts one's *power* over the object by depicting it. A paradigm of enframing in this sense is the representation of the female nude as an object for use, the conversion of the female body into standing reserve in Western art. But much Western pictorial art can be understood along the same lines: it seeks to constitute its object as an object, to push it into a distance from the self and make it available for understanding and use.

Quite the reverse is true in a Taoist conception of art, and of depiction. In order to make a bell stand, Ch'ing must first match his nature to the nature of the trees; he must arrive precisely at the point at which he cannot experience the tree as an object suited to his use, and at which he cannot experience himself as a subject who is able to make use of the tree. This devotion to process and material is what the theory of art given here would lead us to expect from great artists and craftsman; they learn to experience their material as and in themselves. They identify with the material, rather than place the material at a distance.

The most deeply developed art of Taoist China is landscape painting. And here quite clearly we see in the structure of depiction an alternative to enframing. The great seventeenth and eighteenth century landscape painter and monk Shih T'ao (the name means Stone Waves) described his art as follows:

> The ancients were able to express forms through brush and ink and by means of hills and streams, the actions without action and transformation of things without transformation. They left a name for posterity without being well known in their lifetime, for they had gone through the awakening and growth and life, recorded in the work they left behind, and had thus incorporated into themselves the substance of hills and

streams. With regard to ink, the artist has received the function of awakening and growth; with regard to the brush, the function of life; with regard to mountains and rivers, the function of understructure; with regard to contour and surface lines, the function of spontaneity. With regard to the seas and oceans, he has received the function of the universe; with regard to the low backyards, the function of the moment; with regard to no-action, that of action; with regard to the one-stroke, that of all strokes; with regard to the responsive wrist, that of the tip of the brush.[5]

The character of this art is clearly visible in its works. It is often thought, for example, that Chinese landscape painting is marred by the lack of coherent perspective and a single viewpoint. In fact, however, it would be inconsistent with Shih T'ao's conception of art to impose a single viewpoint on the landscape. He does not regard himself as a spectator of mountains, or bamboo, but as mountains and bamboo. When he depicts mountains, he does so from the "point of view" of a mountain. When he depicts water, he "flows," and so does his "viewpoint." And when he depicts human beings, he depicts them as natural objects absorbed in the landscape. The ancients acted in the absence of the illusion of agency; they acted without action. And in order to do that, they had to become identified with the painting and with the things depicted in the painting, or rather, they had to realize that they were already so identified. As Laurence Binyon wrote of a landscape by Wang Wei, a poet and painter of the eighth century:

> Nothing of what to the average mind is beautiful; yet in this foreland scene there was something strangely moving, just because the painter had absorbed the solitude of trees and water into himself. He painted it internally, so to speak, not as something alien and seen from the outside. ... With Chinese, space often becomes a protagonist in the design. It is not final

peace, but itself an activity flowing out from the picture into our minds.[6]

For Shih T'ao, the most astounding products of art reduced to a single movement: this he called the "one-stroke method," or alternately "the method of no method." This method, as the above quotation indicates, involves receiving into oneself the creative power of the things one depicts, and then a letting it flow into the things one uses to depict them with, such as brushes and one's own wrist. One's art is one's participation in *physis*. In his marvelous book *Creativity and Taoism*, Chang Chung-yuan translates a Chinese verse from the eighth century:

The wild geese fly across the long sky above.
Their image is reflected upon the chilly water below.
The geese do not mean to cast their image on the water;
Nor does the water mean to hold the image of the geese.

Chang writes: "This little poem is a metaphor for the idea of reflection as creativity. When the geese fly above the water, they are free of any intention of casting their image upon it, even as the water has no intention of reflecting their flight. But it is at this moment that their beauty is most purely reflected."[7] Reflection, or representation, is part of the Taoist artist's *physis*, something that arises spontaneously into and out of himself.

Representation as enframing is characteristic of and peculiar to the West. If I now give some examples of alternative modes and uses of representations, it is not to assert that the function of representation is the same in the cultures I mention (it most emphatically is not), but simply to develop alternatives to enframing. Two of these alternatives are an identification of the artist or viewer, through representations, with the represented object, and an identification, through (for example) sampling, of the representation itself with the represented object.

In Indian Tantrism images are used for an ecstatic identification with the depicted god, and the image emerges in the first place out of such an identification:

> The identity of the hidden nature of the worshiper with the god worshiped is the first principle of the Tantric philosophy of devotion. . . . [The Tantric initiate] sets before his eyes and mind an image (*pratīka, pratimā*) of the deity. This may be a statue, painting, symbol of some kind, or yantra [geometrical diagram]. . . . The first act of devotion consists in contemplating inwardly the mental image of the deity and then projecting the spiritual energy (*tejas*) of that inner subtle form into the gross outer image.[8]

Or consider again the medicine bundles of the Menominee, which are used, among other things, to aid in hunting:

> The weasels, who are mighty hunters, who run softly like snakes through the grass in summer, and in winter under the snow, they who are always sure of game when they go hunting, they too came to show their good will toward the people, the aunts and uncles of Me'napus [the hero of this myth]. The weasel came to Me'napus and said, "I shall enter by the deer's mouth and pass out of his rectum, I shall kill him as I pass through his vitals," and he sang a song.
>
> "All right, my little brother, you too shall be in the medicine bundle to help my aunts and uncles, the people, to hunt." So Me'napus put the weasel in the bundle, and the weasel's skin may still be found there.[9]

Eventually, the bundle comes to contain tokens of many animals, including the beaver, the mink, birds, and the bear. As well, it contains small representations of the tools of the hunt. It is a device for identification with nature, and the natural process of the hunt in which the animals themselves engage. It is the culture and the spirituality of the Menominee in germ: it encapsulates their veneration of nature and their participation in it by hunting.

Similar bundle representations are created by the Kongo people of Africa. One such bundle, the *Nkisi Nkita Nsumbu*, has the power to "stone the immoral with diseases of the skin, protect the righteous, and create storms."[10] The bundle contains earth, stones, and seeds. Thompson says that it represents the world as a whole. But notice now that the structure of representation here is anything but an enframing. Rather, the *Nkita Nsumbu* represents the world precisely by being and containing part of the world. There is no longer an ontological gap between representation and represented object; representation happens precisely in and through an immersion in reality, rather than by pushing reality off into an aesthetic distance in enframing. In both of these cases, the bundles are employed in the context of wider representative practices: rituals and ceremonies that enact the identification.

In the case of Tantrism, the initiate identifies with the deity through the image. In the case of bundles, the charm comes to represent the hunt, or even the entire world, by containing samples of the world. In the latter case, depiction is not in question at all: the world is used to represent itself. Both of these alternatives to enframing are employed simultaneously in Navajo sings. There, a sand painting of a culture hero is created, and healing is carried out by the identification of the afflicted person with the depiction. But then the identification is carried out by actually applying the sand of which the depiction consists to the person who is to be healed. Once the identification has been made, that is, the picture works as a charm; it is itself effective as a sample of the depicted object.

It is only in the context of aesthetic differentiation—peculiar to the West of modernity—that the work is held to be alienated from process and from what, if anything, it depicts. And it is alienated, too, from itself, from its own ontological status as a real thing the realness of which is necessary to its function as a representation.

However, it might be pointed out here that the account that a person or a society renders to itself about how it makes things is not necessarily the truth about their making. Perhaps even as we attempt to impose a distance between ourselves and the world by "representing" the world pictorially, and even as we try to impose a distance between ourselves and pictures by representing pictures aesthetically (for example, in the philosophy of art), the world and pictures are resisting this treatment. Perhaps, in fact, we retreat into this distance because we find the proximity of things, their impertinence or even cruelty, unbearable. Perhaps this attempt to evade what we depict is the most vivid demonstration that, for us, evasion is impossible. Perhaps our attempt to subdue and utilize the female body in pictures, for example, simply shows that, for we Western men, the female body is that which most indefatigably resists utilization.

IV

So it looks, after all, like an artistic (aesthetic) understanding of art might be false to the essence of art, even as we practice it within the context created by aestheticism. Likewise, it may be that a technological understanding of technology might be false to the essence of technology, even as we practice it within a context that is technologically created. For Taoism, people are things among other things. They are enabled to know and participate in things in virtue of their own thingliness. And as we saw in the last chapter, this insight can ground a profound re-envisioning not only of art but, together with art, of knowledge and action.

The following passage from the *Chuang Tzu* summarizes Taoist epistemology:

> Chuang Tzu and Hui Tzu were strolling along the dam of the Hao River when Chuang Tzu said, "See how the minnows come out and dart around where they please! That's what fish really enjoy!"
>
> Hui Tzu said, "You're not a fish—how do you know what fish enjoy?"

Chuang Tzu said, "You're not I, so how do you know I don't know what fish enjoy?"

Hui Tzu said, "I'm not you, so I certainly don't know what you know. On the other hand, you're certainly not a fish—so that still proves you don't know what fish enjoy!"

Chuang Tzu said, "Let's go back to your original question, please. You asked me *how* I know what fish enjoy—so you already knew I knew it when you asked the question. I know it by standing here beside the Hao." (p. 110)

This is characteristically playful. But it also provides what, from a Western point of view, is a stunning answer to the question "How do you know?" The answer is not: "by representing the fish's activity to myself in a certain way," or "by gathering information on the playful proclivities of fish." Rather, the answer is that Chuang Tzu knows what fish enjoy by *being where* fish are, by being juxtaposed to fish. One knows in identification, in virtue of the fact that one is a thing among things. This is an alternative to enframing as a way of knowing and as a style of art.

That we are subjects by whom objects can be used: that is an illusion. We are always completely a part of what is. Thus, all human creation, including industrial production, is a participation by persons in the coming into appearance of things. All human creation is a poetic participation in the *physis* of things.

This insight might make it possible for us to let go of both the pride and the self-loathing that we experience in the face of technology. We are proud of our power. But the power that resides in the essence of technology, if any, is not ours. We loathe ourselves in our separation from what we conceive to be nature, for imposing artificial transformations on the pristinity of the really real. But it is truer to say that, through us, nature is transforming itself. And it is yet truer to say that the concept of nature is itself technologically articulated, that once that we see that the notion of the artificial is illusory, we will see the same of the natural.

Notes

1. Martin Heidegger, "The Question Concerning Technology," in *Martin Heidegger: Basic Writings*, ed. David Farrell Krell (New York: Harper & Row, 1977), 288, 289.

2. Lao Tzu, *Tao Te Ching*, trans. Gia-fu Feng and Jane English (New York: Random House, 1972), chapter 29.

3. Chuang Tzu, *The Complete Works of Chuang Tzu*, trans. Burton Watson (New York: Columbia University Press, 1968), 204, 205.

4. Kuo Hsiang, *Commentary on the Chuang Tzu*, in *A Source Book in Chinese Philosophy*, ed. Wing-tsit Chan (Princeton: Princeton University Press, 1963), 328.

5. Shih T'ao, "An Expressionist Credo," *The Chinese Theory of Art*, ed. Lin Yutang (London: Heinemann, 1967), 154.

6. Laurence Binyon, *The Spirit of Man in Asian Art*, quoted in Chang Chung-yuan, *Creativity and Taoism* (New York: The Julian Press, 1963), 92, 93.

7. Chang Chung-yuan, *Creativity and Taoism* (New York: The Julian Press, 1963), 57.

8. Heinrich Zimmer, *Philosophies of India* (New York: Meridian, 1956), 581, 582.

9. "Myth and Ritual of a Menominee Medicine Bundle," *Native North American Spirituality of the Eastern Woodlands* (Mahwah, NJ: Paulist Press, 1979), 146.

10. Robert Farris Thompson, *Flash of the Spirit: African and Afro-American Art and Philosophy* (New York: Vintage, 1984), 119.

Concluding Remarks

We already have what we want. If there is one thing in this book that I want to convey as an insight, that is it. This does not mean that there are not things that need to be changed, but it is an expression of hope that we can come to see our world more clearly and appreciate it more deeply. The process of coming to awareness of what we have and what we are is the process of coming to life. And immersion in this process is the art of living. Peace comes in affirming what is: pitting ourselves against the automobile or against heavy metal music or against weaponry is simply a way of pitting ourselves against ourselves: for we, like weapons, are real. And we are the human beings who made these things; we too are things that were made.

Perhaps the deepest experience that any of us can have of fusion is the experience of love. Maybe that is why we think sex is an appropriate expression of love, or at any rate of some love: because sex is a physical fusion. And there is an art of love; or rather, without love there is no art; to engage in an activity out of love for it is to engage in it as an art. That is why throughout human history and all over the world, spiritual traditions have called up, or even consisted of, art. Art, as we have seen, is necessary for ritual, and ritual is necessary to mark passages in lives and in seasons and in eras. Human beings need *markers* along the path, they need to reflect in their own making the making that is going on universally around them. Better, they need to participate with their own bodies in the changes they experience in the world. Ritual is, finally, a way of *being* the world, of showing that the order of culture *is*, always, the order of nature. Art that is culturally connected shows that there is no distinction between the natural and the artificial. And in the fusion that is ritual, a great love is expressed. Even when changes in the world are causes of fear, or pain, or death, we mark our love for these changes in the creation of art. Art shows that we can love the world even in pain and death, that we can love even pain and death.

That does not mean that we stop experiencing pain as pain, or that we stop experiencing loss, or the fear of being lost. On the contrary, we open ourselves to these things completely by means of art. We express in art our willingness to undergo these things. This expression is perverse, because we will undergo these things whether we are willing to or not. But this desire to open ourselves to the world even in the face of the world's cruelty is also a posture of great nobility. To fight against the truth, to wave a fist at fate and the gods who bequeath it, is admirable insofar as fighting is itself admirable. But ultimately such a stance is madness, egomania. To fight against what is—to hate and attack what cannot be avoided— that is perhaps the deepest pain of which human beings are capable. To affirm our world in process does not exempt us from that pain any more than it exempts us from any other, because one of the things that we would have to accept is that we cannot accept everything.

But to engage in an art is to forget about the abstractions and walk into the *work* of making ourselves a home in the universe. We make ourselves a home in one way or another: technologically, spontaneously, or whatever. To engage in an art is to begin to make a home for ourselves—to make ourselves at home in the world—mindfully. It is to heighten our awareness of where and who we are by actually engaging in the world more openly and more devotedly. It is a way of experiencing the sacredness of the mundane; it is a way of consecrating ourselves and our things. Art, finally, is our nature, our way of being real, of making a home and loving the world.

Index